**Char-Broil** TRU. INFRARED
Grilling's Juicy Little Secret™

*grilling*

# CHICKEN
## AND VEGGIES

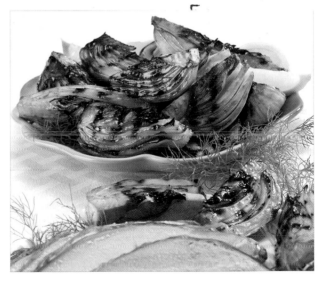

CB's Fire-Charred Green Beans
with Vinaigrette, page 66

CREATIVE
HOMEOWNER®

**Char-Broil®** *Grilling's Juicy Little Secret™* **TRU INFRARED™**

*grilling*

# CHICKEN
## AND VEGGIES

**150** **SAVORY RECIPES FOR SIZZLE ON THE GRILL**

CREATIVE HOMEOWNER®, Upper Saddle River, New Jersey

COPYRIGHT © 2012

# CRE**A**TIVE
## HOMEOWNER®

A Division of Federal Marketing Corp.
Upper Saddle River, NJ

Creative Homeowner® is a registered trademark of Federal Marketing Corporation.

The Big Easy®, Char-Broil® Quantum®, Char-Broil® RED®, and TRU-Infrared™ are registered trademarks of Char-Broil®, LLC. Sizzle on the Grill™ is a trademark of Char-Broil®, LLC.

Nutella® is a registered trademark of Ferrero.

Tabasco® is a registered trademark of the McIlhenny Company.

## Char-Broil GRILLING CHICKEN AND VEGGIES

| | |
|---|---|
| SENIOR EDITOR | Kathie Robitz |
| CONTRIBUTING EDITOR | Barry "CB" Martin |
| PROOFREADER | Sara M. Markowitz |
| INDEXER | Erica Caridio, The Last Word |
| PRINCIPAL PHOTOGRAPHERS | Glenn E. Teitell, Dyne Benner (food stylist), Freeze Frame Studio; Glenn Moores, Trudy Hewer (food stylist), Stuart Marston (grill chef), Contact Jupiter, Inc. (photo coordinator) |
| DIGITAL IMAGING SPECIALIST | Mary Dolan |
| DESIGN AND LAYOUT | David Geer |

### CREATIVE HOMEOWNER

| | |
|---|---|
| VICE PRESIDENT AND PUBLISHER | Timothy O. Bakke |
| MANAGING EDITOR | Fran J. Donegan |
| ART DIRECTOR | David Geer |
| PRODUCTION COORDINATOR | Sara M. Markowitz |

Current Printing (last digit)
10 9 8 7 6 5 4 3 2 1

Manufactured in the United States of America

Char-Broil Grilling Chicken and Veggies, First Edition
Library of Congress Control Number: 2011932132
ISBN-10: 1-58011-545-4
ISBN-13: 978-1-58011-545-2

CREATIVE HOMEOWNER®
A Division of Federal Marketing Corp.
24 Park Way
Upper Saddle River, NJ 07458
**www.creativehomeowner.com**

All photography by
**Glenn E. Teitell and Glenn Moores**
except as noted.

page 17: *left* courtesy Char-Broil;
page 20: courtesy Char-Broil;
page 21: courtesy Char-Broil

# Acknowledgments

We would like to thank the home and professional cooks who have shared some of their recipes in this book. And to those who love backyard cooking, enjoy!

*Indian-Spice Grilled Cauliflower, page 95*

*BBQ Orange Chicken,*
*page 49*

# Contents

CB's Moroccan-Spice Grilled
Chicken & Peaches, page 54

# Introduction

**A diet of chicken and vegetables** can be healthy, but it can get boring unless you've got a variety of tasty recipes such as those in Char-Broil's *Grilling Chicken and Veggies*.

First, chef Barry "CB" Martin offers tips for getting that great grilled taste in Chapter 1, beginning on page 10. For delicious chicken, go to Chapter 2, where you'll find such recipes as "Grilled Yogurt-Mint Chicken," page 34; "Sesame-Crusted Chicken with Wasabi Cream Sauce," page 36; and "CB's Moroccan-Spice Grilled Chicken & Peaches," page 54.

For scrumptious vegetable fare that you can serve as a main course or as an accompaniment to your chicken dish, you'll find "Garlic-Roasted Sweet Potatoes with Arugula," page 76; "Marinated Portobello Mushrooms with Roasted-Pepper Vinaigrette," page 79; and "Indian-Spice Grilled Cauliflower," page 95. But that's just a few of the savory dishes in Chapter 3.

"Becky's Barley Casserole," page 112; "Stuffed Tomatoes on the Grill," page 117; and "Cranberry-Pecan Rice Pilaf," page 125, are among the side dishes featured in Chapter 4. Some of these recipes are perfect alone as light meals or as an added dish to your menu.

If you've got a sweet tooth, you'll enjoy the mouth-watering desserts in Chapter 5. "Tim Barr's Smoked Pears with Berry Compote," page 139, is easy and elegant—serve it and impress your guests. Mom, Dad, and the kids will all love "CB's Nutella & Marshmallow Quesadillas," page 142. For something sweet and light, try "Grilled Pineapple with Yogurt & Walnuts," page 143. It's pure pleasure without the guilt!

Lastly, to make your dishes extra special, check out the marinades, sauces, and rubs in Chapter 6.

Grilled Corn with Sun-Dried
Tomato Pesto, page 86

# 1 Hot off the Grill

*Coffee & Cocoa Grilled Chicken Thighs, page 37*

# Know Your Heat

Searing the meat first prevents chicken parts and other single portions from drying quickly. Searing locks in the juices and produces that delicious crust that makes grilling popular in the first place.

For the most satisfying grilled or barbecued meals, know your heat. You may have heard the terms *direct heat* and *indirect heat*. Understanding these two terms and using these methods is the key to mouth-watering, moist and delicious outdoor cooking.

**GRILLING,** or **DIRECT-HEAT** cooking refers to preparing food directly over the heat source (propane- or natural-gas-powered burners, hot coals, burning wood). This method of cooking is usually at a high temperature. Rotisserie cooking is done by direct heat, too, as is frying a chicken or turkey.

Large, less-tender cuts of meat are best cooked by **INDIRECT HEAT.** This process of slow roasting at a low temperature, or **BARBECUING,** takes longer but adds flavor and tenderness to meat. Using a smoker? Then you're cooking with indirect heat. Sometimes, you might start cooking over direct heat—to brown or sear a piece of meat, for example—and then finish with indirect heat. You'll find references to direct and indirect heat in almost every outdoor cooking recipe.

Finally, don't forget to practice safe food-handling habits, and always start with cleanliness (page 20). And always start with a clean grill (page 21). For additional temperature guidelines, see page 25.

1

# Poultry Cooking-Temperature Table

| MEAT | TEMPERATURE | VISUAL DESCRIPTION |
| --- | --- | --- |
| | USDA guidelines | |
| General poultry | 165°F | Cook until juices run clear. |
| Whole chicken | 165°F | Cook until juices run clear and leg moves easily. |
| Parts of chicken | 165°F | Cook until juices run clear. |

NOTE: *Always cook poultry to at least the temperatures recommended by the United States Department of Agriculture to prevent food-borne illness. However, some parts of poultry, such as legs and thighs, cooked to 165°F, while safe, would be considered undercooked by many people. Consult individual recipes for finish cooking temperatures.*

# Smoking

Smoking is the process of cooking food between 140°F and 225°F over or near an open fire made from wood or charcoal. The fire releases particles of these materials into the smoker that impart a unique flavor to the meat. The more these materials smolder and generate smoke, the greater the number of particles to flavor the food. Cooking at temperatures of 225°F–350°F is called **HOT SMOKING.**

If the smoke passes through a cooling chamber and comes into contact with the food at a temperature of around 45°F, you are **COLD SMOKING** the food. (Note: cold-smoked food isn't actually cooked, it's simply being slow-cured and flavored.)

When moisture is added to the smoker to increase its humidity level, it is called **WET SMOKING.** A simple pan of water is placed away from direct heat inside the grill or smoker. If desired, you can use fruit juice or wine instead of water, or add these liquids to the water for an additional flavor boost.

**Smoker Box** (shown on top of grates for clarity)

**"Smoke Bomb"**

**Wood Chips**

**Smoking with wood or charcoal on a charcoal grill such as Char-Broil's CB940 uses indirect heat.**

# Infrared Cooking: What Is It and How Does It Work?

Infrared is a natural form of radiant heat we've all experienced in our daily lives. The warm rays of the sun are transferred to your skin by infrared heat waves. And if you've ever made "sun tea," you've brewed it using the sun's infrared heat.

Charcoal, used to cook food for centuries, is still prized today for the flavor it imparts to food. The infrared heat produced by the charcoal is the key to helping food retain its juiciness and flavor. However, charcoal fires require more time and effort to adequately prepare them for grilling.

With the introduction of an affordable line of gas grills equipped with infrared, Char-Broil has made the technology used for decades by professional chefs available to backyard grillers. You'll find this exciting technology in Char-Broil's new TRU-Infrared line of grills. Any product displaying the TRU-Infrared badge guarantees unparalleled infrared performance.

## HOW IT WORKS

Infrared heat is a great way to cook. This method generates higher temperatures for faster cooking and uses less fuel. Preventing flare-ups, and delivering even heat with no hot spots, means much juicier foods.

So, how does it work? Infrared waves start to cook the food the instant they reach its surface, preserving the moisture barrier and quickly locking in natural juices and flavors while giving you exceptional browning.

Char-Broil's TRU-Infrared cooking system offers a wide temperature range, from a searing high heat to a low and slow heat for barbecuing and rotisserie grilling.

Since flare-ups are prevented, you can simply drop wood chips on or between your grill's grates to create a slow-cooked smokehouse flavor in a fraction of the time.

**Char-Broil's Commercial grills use TRU-Infrared technology that gives you juicier food and eliminates flare-ups and hot or cold spots.**

## INFRARED COOKING TIPS

Experience with your new infrared grill will help you determine what temperatures and cooking times deliver the best results. At first, you may want to adjust your regular cooking times. If you have cooked on a charcoal fire, this should be fairly easy to do. If you are more familiar with cooking on a regular convection gas grill, reduce the heat settings you normally use by at least 30 percent, and the cooking time by about 50 percent. Here are some other ideas that will help you master infrared cooking:

→ Coat each piece of food with a light spray of high-heat oil, such as canola.

→ Plan your cooking according to technique, required times, and the best use of the grill surface. For example, steaks can be seared over high heat then finished over medium or low heat. Begin with steaks you intend to cook to medium doneness, and end with those you want rare.

# Oil-Free "Frying"

The Big Easy Oil-less Turkey Fryer is a safe way to "fry" a turkey or cook rotisserie-style chicken.  Pork loin, roast beef, or vegetables turn out great with the same TRU-infrared(™) technology. And you can use dry rubs and seasonings on the outside of the bird, unlike with traditional fryers.

1. Brine the bird up to 24 hours for extra flavor.

2. Spray cooking basket with vegetable oil.

3. Place bird—breast facing up—in the basket.

4. Allow the bird to rest for 20 to 30 minutes.

# Spit Roasting

Rotisserie cooking is yet another way to roast large pieces of meat or poultry. A rotating spit driven by an electric or battery-powered motor is set directly over the heat source and turns at a constant, consistent speed to allow for even cooking. Use an instant-read thermometer inserted into the deepest part of the food to check for doneness—just be sure to stop the rotisserie motor first. It's also a good idea to wear heat-resistant gloves when you're removing the spit rod from the grill.

**In addition to large roasts, a rotisserie cooks whole poultry over direct heat.**

# CB's Secrets for Great Taste

**JUICY CHICKEN**

I may not be the world's authority on grilling chicken, but I do enjoy preparing and eating it. And over the years, I've acquired a few tricks that help ensure the most lip-smacking results.

**BUY FRESH CHICKEN.** Buy the best quality you can afford, and fresh is best. I've also taken to using organic chickens because I think they taste more like the chickens I remember eating as a kid.

**TO BRINE OR NOT TO BRINE.** My mom liked to tenderize chicken by soaking it overnight in buttermilk. Brine will produce the same results, and help retain juiciness. (See "CB's Basic Brine Recipe" on page 157.)

**SEASONING.** Apply sauces and glazes during the final minutes of cooking. If you like the taste of a dry rub, check the ingredient list before using. Many spices will burn when exposed to high temperatures, which can ruin the flavor. I recommend only a light seasoning of ground pepper, as well as kosher salt if the chicken hasn't been brined. You can also lightly spray chicken with canola oil to prevent sticking.

**TEMPERATURE AND TIME.** First, make sure to remove your chicken from the refrigerator and let it warm up for just a few minutes before cooking. Be careful never to let raw poultry reach room temperature, but try to avoid putting ice-cold chicken on the grill because that interferes with proper cooking.

The second most important rule for grilling chicken is to cook it from the inside out. The USDA recommends an internal temperature of 165°F for both chicken parts and whole chickens. Use an instant-read thermometer to gauge the internal temperature of the meat, making sure to keep the probe away from bones. If you cook chicken using the four-stage method suggested below, you can test the temperature at each stage.

Some things to remember: dark meat takes longer to cook than white meat; and larger pieces take longer to cook than smaller ones. The legs and thighs are dark meat. The wings, drumettes, and breast are white meat. Start cooking dark-meat chicken parts first. If you are cooking chicken halves, start them bone side down to speed up cooking.

**STAGE 1: SEARING (450°F–550°F).** This temperature range is perfect for searing steaks, but it's also a great place to start grilling chicken. A quick sear on both sides will help to lock in natural juices and flavor.

**STAGE 2: GRILLING (350°F–450°F).** On one half of the grill, set the heat to medium high (about 500°F). Set the heat to medium low (about 375°F) on the other half. Start by placing fresh pieces of chicken on the hotter side. After searing for just a short time (2 to 3 minutes on an infrared grill, longer on a standard grill) the chicken will begin to get grill marks.

Although flare-ups on Char-Broil's infrared gas grills are rare, you may need to watch for them on other grills. Using your instant-read thermometer, check the chicken's internal temperature. Look for a temperature of approximately 145°F to 155°F to move from grilling to glazing.

**STAGE 3: GLAZING (200°F).** During the final ten minutes of cooking, reduce the heat under the chicken to low, and glaze the chicken with sauce. I like to use apricot or peach marmalade depending upon what else is on the menu. Whatever your taste dictates, the chicken should be almost fully cooked and removed from any direct heat before glazing. For perfect glazing, simmer the sauce before brushing it on the meat.

**STAGE 4: REST, REST, REST.** When you're finished grilling, place all of the chicken in trays or foil pans; cover; and let it rest for at least 10 minutes. This will help redistribute the juices inside each piece and allow the internal temperature to rise an additional 5 to 10 degrees. If you like, you may also add more sauce.

## DELICIOUS VEGETABLES

Grilling vegetables requires little preparation and imparts a delicious, lightly smoked flavor.

→ Set a standard gas grill to high; an infrared grill to medium high.

→ Lightly brush or spray vegetables with olive oil before grilling to add flavor, promote sear marks, and keep them from sticking to the grill.

→ Some vegetables, such as corn on the cob, mushrooms, and baby eggplants, can be grilled whole. Others, such as zucchini, bell peppers, and onions, should be sliced or cut into wedges.

→ Start vegetables over medium-high heat to sear their skins, turning every 1 to 2 minutes. Then move to low heat to finish cooking, turning occasionally.

→ The easiest way to tell whether vegetables are cooked or not is to pierce them with a fork or skewer. If it goes in easily, the vegetables are done.

## GRILLED FRUIT FOR DESSERT

Lightly grilling fruit—especially stone fruits, such as peaches, nectarines, apricots, and plums—caramelizes their natural sugars, enhances their flavor, and provides appetizing grill marks.

→ Set a standard gas grill to high; an infrared grill to medium.

→ Generously oil grill grate to avoid sticking.

→ Slice fruit in half, and remove pits. Grill with pulp side down, turning once, until tender, about 3 to 5 minutes.

→ Fruit is done when it is lightly browned and tender but not mushy.

→ Fruit can burn easily because of its sugar content, so watch it closely.

→ Cut fruit, such as apples, pears, mangoes, pineapples, and peaches, into chunks and brush lightly with canola oil before grilling. Put pineapple or bananas sliced lengthwise directly on the grill.

**1**

**Hot off the Grill**

# Good Grilling Hygiene

I can't overemphasize the importance of good grilling hygiene. The food you serve to your family and friends must be wholesome as well as tasty. By adopting safe food-handling practices in your kitchen—and outside at your grill—you can significantly decrease your risk of food-borne illness.

### WASH UP!

Wash your hands thoroughly with hot water and antibacterial soap, especially after handling raw meat. Better yet, consider using food-safe disposable gloves—they're great for handling hot chili peppers, too. Be sure to toss them away before moving on to other tasks.

If you're using a paper towel to wipe up excess moisture from poultry, dispose of it immediately when you're done. Sterilize a damp sponge in the microwave, set on high, for about 60 seconds or more until it becomes hot. Then let it cool before you grab it, or use tongs to remove it. Launder dish towels and rags in hot water.

Plastic cutting boards can be thrown in the dishwasher. Use several color-coded boards—one for raw poultry, one for vegetables, one for cooked food, and so forth—to prevent cross-contamination. And don't forget to sanitize the sink. Pour diluted bleach down the drain or waste-disposal unit to kill any lingering bacteria, especially after preparing raw meat.

*CB's Chicken with Rosemary Butter & White BBQ Sauce, page 31*

**Keep separate cutting boards for cooked and uncooked foods.**

*Grilled Polenta, page 111*

**Make this delicious side dish on a clean grill for the best taste.**

## A CLEAN GRILL

Burned gunk on the grates is not "seasoning." It's just old, dirty food and will add bad flavors to your next grilled meal. Take care of your grill's grates as you would a favorite cast-iron pan by preseasoning them before the first use. (Refer to your product manual for complete instructions.)

If you don't own one of Char-Broil's infrared gas grills with a built-in self-cleaning feature, here's a secret: fold a large piece of heavy-duty aluminum foil into three layers, forming a sheet that measures about 11 × 24 inches. (A disposable foil tray also works well.) Place the sheet on the grates immediately after grilling. Keep the heat turned on high on a gas grill, or lower the grates on a charcoal grill until they are just about touching the coals. The foil concentrates the heat on the grates, which helps to burn off any cooking residue. The stuff usually turns to a white ash that is easy to brush off once the grates are cool again. Follow this by spritzing the grates with a little canola oil spray to season.

# Check the Temperature

Uh, oh! Did you forget to defrost that package of chicken thighs you were going to grill for dinner? Should you run hot water over it to thaw it quickly? What if you remembered to take the chicken out of the freezer but left the package on the counter all day while you were at work?

Both of these scenarios are bad news. As soon as food begins to defrost and become warmer than 40°F, any bacteria that may have been present before freezing can begin to multiply. So, even though the center of those chicken thighs may still be frozen as they thaw on the counter, the outer layer of the food is in the danger zone. Maintain the temperature of frozen foods at under 0°F, and raw, unfrozen foods at under 40°F.

For hot foods, the minimum safe-holding temperature is above 140°F. Food can certainly pass through this temperature zone during cooking, but if it does not rise above 140°F, you are flirting with bacteria growth that will make you sick. Use an accurate meat thermometer.

As a rule of thumb, chicken breasts, as well as ground poultry, should be cooked to at least 165°F.

See the cooking temperature guidelines on page 25 for more specific information.

Barbecued Chicken Thighs au Vin, page 42

**Cook these thighs until the juices run clear.**

# How to Safely Defrost Foods

There are three safe ways to defrost food: in the refrigerator, in cold water, and in the microwave.

### REFRIGERATOR THAWING

Planning ahead is the key. A large frozen turkey requires at least a day (24 hours) for every 5 pounds of weight. Even a pound of boneless chicken breasts needs a full day to thaw. Remember, there may be different temperature zones in your refrigerator, and food left in the coldest one will take longer to defrost.

After thawing in the refrigerator, poultry can be chilled for an additional day or two before cooking. You can also refreeze uncooked foods that have been defrosted in the refrigerator, but there may be some loss of flavor and texture.

### COLD-WATER THAWING

This method is faster than refrigerator thawing but requires more attention. Place the food in a leak-proof plastic bag, and submerge it in cold tap water. Change the water every 30 minutes until the food is defrosted. Small packages of poultry—about 1 pound—may defrost in an hour or less. For whole turkeys, estimate about 30 minutes per pound. Cook the food immediately after it defrosts. You can refreeze the cooked food.

### MICROWAVE THAWING

This is the speediest method, but it can be uneven, leaving some areas of the food still frozen and others partially cooked. The latter can reach unsafe temperatures if you do not completely cook the food immediately. Foods thawed in the microwave should be cooked before refreezing.

# Safety Check for Grills

As I cruise around my neighborhood, I often notice grills on apartment terraces and backyard decks, and I get the chills. Why? Because many of these devices are way too close to wooden railings, siding, and fences. Regardless of the type of cooker you own, keep it at least 3 feet from any wall or surface, and 10 feet from other flammable objects. Here are some other tips for safe outdoor cooking from the Hearth, Patio & Barbecue Association.

**→ READ THE OWNER'S MANUAL.** Follow its specific recommendations for assembly, usage, and safety procedures. Contact the manufacturer if you have questions. For quick reference, write down the model number and customer-service phone number on the cover of your manual.

**→ KEEP OUTDOOR GRILLS OUTDOORS.** Never use them to cook in your trailer, tent, house, garage, or any enclosed area because toxic carbon monoxide may accumulate.

**→ GRILL IN A WELL-VENTILATED AREA.** Set up your grill in a well-ventilated, open area that is away from buildings, overhead combustible surfaces, dry leaves, or brush. Avoid high-traffic areas, and be aware of wind-blown sparks.

**→ KEEP IT STABLE.** Always check to be sure that all parts of the unit are firmly in place and that the grill can't tip.

**→ FOLLOW ELECTRICAL CODES.** Electric accessories, such as some rotisseries, must be properly grounded in accordance with local codes. Keep electric cords away from walkways or anywhere people can trip over them.

**→ USE LONG-HANDLED UTENSILS.** Long-handled forks, tongs, spatulas, and such are designed to help you avoid burns and splatters when you're grilling food.

**→ WEAR SAFE CLOTHING.** That means no hanging shirttails, frills, or apron strings that can catch fire, and use heat-resistant mitts when adjusting hot vents.

**→ KEEP FIRE UNDER CONTROL.** To put out flare-ups, lower the burners to a cooler temperature (or either raise the grid that is supporting the food or spread coals out evenly, or both, for charcoal). If you must douse flames, do it with a light spritz of water after removing the food from the grill. Keep a fire extinguisher handy in case there is a grease fire. If you don't have one, keep a bucket of sand nearby.

**→ INSTALL A GRILL PAD OR SPLATTER MAT UNDER YOUR GRILL.** These naturally heat-resistant pads are usually made of lightweight fiber cement or plastic and will protect your deck or patio from any grease that misses the drip pan.

**→ NEVER LEAVE A LIT GRILL UNATTENDED.** Furthermore, don't attempt to move a hot grill, and always keep kids and pets away when the grill is in use and for up to an hour afterward.

**1**

Hot off the Grill

Smoky Baby Blue Artichokes, page 65

# Keep These Handy

## CB'S PANTRY

→ **PURE VEGETABLE OIL/COOKING OIL SPRAY.** This is an essential tool for lubricating meat and grill grates.

→ **COARSE SALT.** The larger crystals of coarse salt are wonderful because you can actually see where you have salted.

→ **GARLIC** (granulated and fresh). This is a basic flavor for most grilling sauces and rubs.

→ **CUMIN.** This spice is the secret of all great barbecue cooks.

→ **ONIONS** (powdered, granulated, or fresh). You'll find that onions enhance most every barbecue recipe.

→ **APPLE CIDER VINEGAR.** This provides the flavor of apple cider without the sugar and is the choice of most master grillers. Use by itself as a spray or as a liquid component of wet rubs, mops, and sauces.

→ **KETCHUP.** This versatile ingredient can be combined with many others to form a quick sauce.

→ **BROWN SUGAR.** I use it for dry rubs. When combined with ketchup, it creates a sweet glaze for chicken.

CHAR-BROIL SPICE STICK

Model #4984300

## CB'S MUST-HAVE GRILLING TOOLS

→ **KNIVES.** A good knife is essential to prepping and carving meat. I recommend you choose knives that feel good in your hand, work for different tasks, can be used outdoors, don't cost a fortune, and are easy to clean and sharpen.

→ **SPATULA.** I've tried all styles and price points, and my favorite has a wooden handle with a sturdy blade that supports a good-sized piece of meat, and easily slides between the grate and the food.

→ **TONGS.** I buy tongs in a variety of colors to indicate their purpose. I use red ones for raw meat and black ones for meat that's cooked.

→ **FORK.** I primarily use the fork with the tongs and spatula when I need a little extra help. I almost never use it to poke or turn meat.

→ **BASTING BRUSH.** I am so grateful to the person who invented silicone cooking utensils. This type of brush is my mainstay. The angle is great for getting to places without twisting my wrist, and the brush holds sauce and clarified butter quite well.

→ **THERMOMETERS.** The most important thermometer I own is a pocket instant-read thermometer. They are very useful for quickly testing meat in various areas to see if it's cooking evenly.

Char-Broil offers a remote digital thermometer that has both a food probe and a dangling device that reads the temperature right near the grates. It alerts me if the temperature inside the smoker starts to drop, and it keeps me informed of the internal temperature of the meat.

→ **HEAT-RESISTANT LEATHER GLOVES.** These bad boys are intended for heavy industrial use and can take sparks, heat, and hot metal. They aren't intended for playing in the fire but are very useful when you need to move hot grates and cast-iron pans, and when working around your grill, smoker, or barbecue.

# Grilling Temperature Guidelines

| METHOD OF HEAT | GRATE TEMPERATURE RANGE | DESCRIPTIVE LANGUAGE MOST OFTEN USED |
| --- | --- | --- |
| Direct | Approx. 450°F to 650°F and higher | Sear, searing, or grilling on high |
| Direct | Approx. 350°F to 450°F | Grilling on medium |
| Direct | Approx. 250°F to 350°F | Grilling on low |

# Rotisserie Temperature Guidelines

| METHOD OF HEAT | BURNER TEMPERATURE RANGE | DESCRIPTIVE LANGUAGE MOST OFTEN USED |
| --- | --- | --- |
| Direct | Approx. 350°F to 450°F | Rotisserie or "spit" roasting |

# Roasting Temperature Guidelines

| METHOD OF HEAT | COOKING CHAMBER TEMPERATURE RANGE | DESCRIPTIVE LANGUAGE MOST OFTEN USED |
| --- | --- | --- |
| Indirect | Approx. 350°F to 450°F | Indirect grilling or indirect cooking |
| Indirect | Approx. 250°F to 350°F | Indirect grilling or indirect cooking, "low and slow" |

# Smoking Temperature Guidelines

| METHOD OF HEAT | COOKING CHAMBER TEMPERATURE RANGE | DESCRIPTIVE LANGUAGE MOST OFTEN USED |
| --- | --- | --- |
| Indirect, with wood smoke | Approx. 225°F to 350°F | Hot smoking "low and slow" |
| Indirect, with wood smoke | Approx. 140°F to 225°F | Smoking "low and slow" |

**30**

**36**

**38**

**40**

**42**

**47**

**48**

**54**

**56**

# 2 Chicken

# CB's Grilled Chicken with Balsamic Garlic Sauce

**5 chicken-leg quarters**
**Sea salt and fresh cracked pepper**
**Canola oil spray**

Preheat one side of the grill to medium and the other side to low. Season the chicken with salt and pepper, and lightly spray all sides with canola oil.

Sear the chicken over medium heat, about 3 to 5 minutes per side; then remove it to a foil pan on the low-heat side of the grill. Keep the other side of the grill on medium, but shut off the burners under the pan. Close the lid. Cook until the temperature of the thick thigh meat is 180°F.

**Sauce:** Heat 1 tablespoon of olive oil and the butter in a saucepan over medium-high heat. Add the shallot, cooking until translucent, and then add the garlic. Combine with the vinegar and chicken broth, and bring to a boil.

In a small bowl, mix 1 tablespoon olive oil and flour. Drizzle it into the sauce mixture, whisking to prevent lumps. Bring to a boil; then simmer on low for 1 to 2 minutes, whisking as necessary. Serve with the chicken. Top with the chopped parsley. ✦

## SAUCE
**2 tablespoons olive oil**
**1 tablespoon butter, softened**
**1 small shallot, chopped**
**3 cloves of garlic, minced**
**⅓ cup balsamic vinegar**
**1 cup chicken broth**
**2 tablespoons instant flour**
**Chopped parsley for garnish**

# Catalan Grilled Chicken Legs

4 chicken-leg quarters

¼ teaspoon cayenne pepper

½ teaspoon cumin

½ teaspoon cinnamon

1 teaspoon salt

¼ teaspoon black pepper

2 tablespoons olive oil

1 medium size onion, chopped

4 cloves garlic, chopped

¾ cup chorizo or other spicy sausage, chopped

1 28-ounce can whole, peeled tomatoes, drained and chopped

½ cup full-bodied red wine

½ cup chopped pitted black olives

6 tablespoons pine nuts, toasted

Preheat the grill to high. In a small bowl, stir together the cayenne pepper, cumin, cinnamon, salt, and black pepper. Rub thoroughly over chicken-leg quarters. Reduce grill to medium. Place chicken on grill, and cook, turning until browned on all sides, about 10 minutes. While the chicken is grilling, warm the olive oil in a large pot over medium heat. Add the onions and garlic, and sauté until they begin to brown, about 4 minutes. Stir in the sausage, and continue to sauté for 3 more minutes. Stir in the tomatoes and wine, and bring the mixture to a simmer. When chicken is finished grilling, add it to the pot. Stir in the olives. Cover; reduce heat to medium low; and simmer for 20 minutes.

To serve, put one piece of chicken in each of four shallow bowls. Top with the sauce, and sprinkle with toasted pine nuts. ♣

2

Chicken

# CB's Korean-Style Chicken

3 pounds boneless, skinless chicken
    thighs

⅓ cup soy sauce

2 tablespoons sugar

1 tablespoon sweet rice wine

½ medium onion, grated

2 cloves garlic, mashed and minced

1 teaspoon grated ginger

1 teaspoon Chinese-style dry
    mustard powder

¼ teaspoon black pepper

1 teaspoon sesame seeds, toasted
    for garnish

Green onions or chives, chopped
    for garnish

Flatten chicken thighs. Mix the next eight ingredients in a large plastic bag. Add chicken, and seal. Place the sealed bag in the refrigerator for 1 hour.

About 30 minutes before grilling, remove chicken from marinade. Pat chicken dry, and cover loosely with plastic wrap. Preheat grill to high; then lower one side to medium.

Spray the chicken with canola oil. Sear one side of it over high heat. Then move the chicken, seared side up, to the medium side of the grill. When the chicken reaches an internal temperature just below 160°F, remove it to a foil tray or pan, and put it back on the medium side of the grill. Brush on the glaze, and loosely cover the pan with foil. Chicken is ready when it reaches an internal temperature of 180°F.

Arrange the grilled chicken on a platter, and drizzle with glazing sauce. ✤

## GLAZE

¼ cup soy sauce

1 tablespoon sesame oil

1 tablespoon butter, melted

Mix glaze ingredients
together in a small bowl
and set aside.

# CB's Chicken with Rosemary Butter & White BBQ Sauce

- 2 4- to 5-pound chickens, each cut in half along the back- and breast-bone
- ¼ cup kosher salt
- ¼ cup brown sugar
- 1 tablespoon apple cider vinegar (optional)
- ¼ pound unsalted butter, softened
- Freshly ground sea salt to taste
- Freshly ground black pepper to taste
- ½ cup finely chopped fresh rosemary, plus several sprigs for garnish

Brine chicken, overnight if possible, in a mixture of ¼ cup kosher salt, ¼ cup brown sugar, vinegar, and water to cover. One hour before grilling, remove the chicken; rinse under cool water; and pat dry. Allow the chicken halves to air dry in the fridge for up to several hours if time permits.

Mix butter, salt, pepper, and all but about 2 tablespoons of the rosemary; insert under the skin. Set up your grill for indirect cooking with a drip pan under the grates on the side without heat. Turn on the direct-heat burner. The hood temperature inside the closed grill should read about 400°F.

Place the chicken halves skin side up on the indirect-heat side of the grill, and close the hood. After 15 minutes, move the chicken so that all of it is exposed equally to the "hot" side of the grill. Then turn it over (skin side down) to sear. Continue to cook chicken with the hood closed about another 15 to 20 minutes.

When chicken temperature reaches 160°F, finish cooking, indirectly until internal temperature is 180°F. Drizzle with CB's White BBQ Sauce ✤

**2 Chicken**

## CB'S WHITE BBQ SAUCE

- 1⅓ cups mayonnaise
- 2 garlic cloves, finely minced
- ½ cup fresh lemon juice
- 2 to 3 tablespoons lemon zest (or very finely chopped lemon peel)
- ¼ teaspoon smoked paprika

In a nonreactive bowl, whisk together the ingredients in the order listed. Spoon sauce over hot pieces of grilled chicken or pork.

# Peach-Barbecued Chicken

4 boneless, skinless chicken
   breasts
2 teaspoons onion salt
⅓ cup peach or apricot
   preserves
3 tablespoons barbecue sauce

**SERVE WITH**
**Store-bought buttermilk biscuits**
**Carrot salad**

*Georgia is known as the "peach state" because the commercial peach industry originated there with the introduction of the delectable—and shippable—Elberta peach in 1875.*

Sprinkle chicken with 1 teaspoon onion salt. Combine peach preserves, barbecue sauce, and remaining teaspoon of onion salt in a small bowl.

Grill chicken over medium-low heat, turning and brushing frequently with peach barbecue sauce, for 15 to 20 minutes or until the internal temperature is 165°F. ✚

# CB's Grilled Chicken Cacciatore

2 to 3 pounds chicken thighs and drumsticks
Kosher salt and freshly ground black pepper
3 tablespoons canola oil or spray
1 yellow onion, sliced
2 medium shallots, diced
2 cups diced red, yellow, and/or green peppers
3 cloves garlic, minced
3 tablespoons flour
½ pound mushrooms, quartered
1 cup baby carrots
15-ounce can diced tomatoes
2 cups chicken broth
⅓ cup red wine
2 tablespoons chopped fresh cilantro
2 tablespoons chopped fresh parsley
1 tablespoon dried thyme
¼ teaspoon red pepper flakes
Dash Tabasco sauce
Sliced black olives, if desired

2

Chicken

Preheat grill to high. Season chicken with salt and pepper. Brush or lightly spray chicken with oil. Place on hot grill skin-side down. Cook until browned on one side; then turn and brown the other side, but do not cook completely. Set aside.

Turn grill's side burner to high. In a large, non-reactive pan over the burner, heat the oil. Then reduce heat to medium, and add onion. Sauté for 2 to 3 minutes; add shallots. Continue to cook for 1 minute before adding bell peppers. When shallots and onions begin to caramelize and peppers soften, add garlic, making sure that mixture does not burn.

Add the flour to mixture 1 tablespoon at a time. Add mushrooms and the remaining ingredients.

Reduce heat to low, and add chicken. Cover and cook over indirect heat on grill for 3 to 4 hours. ✤

*Grilling the chicken adds a rich flavor that's even better if you use some wood chips to impart a bit of smoke. To get a head start, grill the chicken the day before.—CB*

# Grilled Yogurt-Mint Chicken

**1 whole chicken, cut
into pieces**

**1 cup plain yogurt**

**6 tablespoons olive oil**

**4 cloves garlic, minced**

**1 cup chopped fresh
mint**

**Salt and pepper**

**Vegetable oil (for the
grill)**

In a large bowl, whisk together the yogurt, olive oil, garlic, mint, and a sprinkling of salt and pepper. Set aside some of the marinade in a separate bowl. Submerge the chicken in the marinade; cover; and refrigerate for 2 to 6 hours.

If using a gas grill, preheat one side to high and one side to low. Oil the grates.

Remove the chicken from the marinade, and season generously with salt and pepper. Put the chicken pieces on the high-heat side of the grill. Let them cook until dark brown grill marks form, 4 to 6 minutes. Turn the chicken, and brown on the other side for 4 to 6 minutes.

Once seared, move the chicken pieces to the low-heat side, and cook until the internal temperature reaches 180°F in thighs. Serve with the reserved sauce. ✤

# CB's Beer-Brined Chicken Quarters

4 chicken quarters (legs and thighs)

1 quart water

¼ cup kosher salt

¼ cup packed brown sugar

12 ounces beer

## RUB

1 tablespoon smoked paprika

1 tablespoon kosher salt

1 teaspoon garlic powder

1 teaspoon ground ginger

1 teaspoon powdered mustard

½ teaspoon pepper

Thoroughly mix together all rub ingredients, and set aside.

Brine the chicken in the water, salt, sugar, and beer, adding the water last to ensure that the chicken is covered. Store in the refrigerator up to 8 hours.

Remove chicken from brine; rinse; and pat dry with paper towels. Refrigerate uncovered about 1 hour to air dry.

Remove chicken from the refrigerator, and apply the rub, massaging it into the skin using your hands in food-safe gloves.

Preheat half of grill to medium high. Spray chicken lightly on all sides with canola oil. Cook chicken pieces on the hot section of the grill until they lift easily and sear marks appear. Turn and sear the other sides.

Move chicken to an aluminum pan on an unheated section of grates; loosely cover with foil; and close grill hood. Reduce the heat to low on the section furthest from the chicken. Cook, covered, until chicken reaches an internal temperature of 180°F. ♣

**2**

Chicken

*Brining is usually done with salted water, in which sugar and assorted flavors have been added. Brining helps the chicken stay moist when grilling.*—CB

# Sesame-Crusted Chicken with Wasabi Cream Sauce

4 boneless, skinless chicken breasts

1 cup bottled teriyaki sauce

½ to 1 teaspoon prepared wasabi*

½ cup light sour cream

2 teaspoons lemon juice

½ teaspoon grated lemon rind

¼ cup black sesame seeds**

¼ cup white sesame seeds

1 egg white, lightly beaten

*Wasabi is Japanese horseradish. It is green and spicy. Prepared wasabi is a ready-to-use paste that comes in a tube. Add more or less wasabi depending on your desire for heat.*

**Black sesame seeds are available at Asian grocery stores. If you prefer, use ½ cup of white sesame seeds instead.*

Pound chicken until slightly flattened. Marinate chicken in the teriyaki overnight in the refrigerator.

Stir wasabi, sour cream, lemon juice, and rind until smooth. Cover and refrigerate until serving time. Preheat the grill to medium. Mix black and white sesame seeds on a plate. Remove chicken from teriyaki sauce; pat it dry using paper towels.

Dip each piece in beaten egg white; then coat with sesame seeds, pressing the seeds into the chicken. Transfer chicken to a wax-paper-lined pan to stand for 10 minutes to allow the coating to set. Grill for 5 to 7 minutes per side with the lid down or until a meat thermometer reads 165°F. Serve immediately with wasabi cream sauce on the side. ✦

# Coffee & Cocoa Grilled Chicken Thighs

8 pieces skinless chicken thighs, bone-in

1 tablespoon plus 2 teaspoons paprika

1 tablespoon chili powder

½ teaspoon sea salt

½ teaspoon sugar

½ teaspoon ground cumin

½ teaspoon ground coriander

½ teaspoon freshly ground black pepper

½ teaspoon garlic powder

1 tablespoon finely ground dark-roast coffee

1 tablespoon cocoa or a dark hot-chocolate mix

Combine spice ingredients in a sealable plastic bag. Add chicken pieces, and shake to coat. Massage spices into the chicken through bag. Allow the chicken to rest for at least 1 hour so that the spice flavors can set. Preheat grill to medium high. Grill, turing often, until a thermometer inserted into the chicken pieces reads 180°F.

Note: use this easy barbecue rub to fully seal chicken pieces to yield the juiciest chicken. Use a strong, dark, powdered coffee, such as espresso, and a high-quality cocoa or hot chocolate. ♣

**2**

# Grilled Chicken Marsala

*Recipe courtesy of www.danicasdaily.com*

4 4-ounce boneless, skinless
    chicken breasts
16 small carrots, peeled
2 teaspoons extra-virgin olive oil
8 ounces sliced fresh mushrooms
2 shallots, chopped
3 cloves garlic, minced
12 ounces Marsala wine or
    low-sodium chicken broth,
    or 6 ounces of each
1 teaspoon cornstarch (optional)
4 tablespoons nonfat yogurt
Chives, chopped for garnish
4 sprigs fresh rosemary

Combine spice mixture, and sprinkle over the chicken. Boil carrots for about 8 to 10 minutes; drain.

Add the oil to a large skillet, and heat over medium heat. Add mushrooms, shallots, and garlic. Season with salt and pepper. Cook until the mushrooms are slightly brown and soft. Add wine or broth. If thicker sauce is desired, stir in cornstarch, and simmer until liquid thickens and reduces to one-third, about 20 minutes.

Preheat grill to medium high. Grill chicken for 8 to 10 minutes on each side or until cooked through. Grill carrots for about 5 minutes, rotating until charred.

Once the mushroom sauce has reduced, remove from heat, and whisk in yogurt. Divide carrots among four plates, and top each with chicken, sauce, chives, and rosemary. ✤

## SPICE MIXTURE

1 teaspoon chopped fresh rosemary
1 teaspoon sea salt
¼ teaspoon freshly ground black pepper
½ teaspoon red pepper flakes

*Grilled Stuffed Tomatoes
    Caprese, page 127*

*I love Marsala sauce, but the traditional version is packed with fat. This lighter recipe has so much creamy, wine-y, mushroom flavor.—CB*

4 Servings • Prep: 20 min. • Marinate: 2 hr.–overnight • Grill: 10 min.

39

# Grilled Stuffed Chicken Breasts with Artichokes & Italian Cheeses

4 large, boneless, skinless chicken breasts

1 bottle Italian salad dressing

2 tablespoons olive oil

1 teaspoon thyme, dried or fresh

¼ teaspoon red pepper flakes

2 cloves garlic, minced

2 tablespoons chopped fresh basil

1 small jar (6 or 7 ounces) artichoke hearts, rinsed and drained

¼ teaspoon salt

A few grinds of pepper

1 cup shredded Italian cheese such as Parmesan, Romano, mozzarella, provolone, or a blend

8 toothpicks

*This recipe for grilled stuffed chicken breasts has just a few more steps than that for a standard chicken breast, but it's a real treat of flavors that keep the chicken juicy.*

Using a sharp paring knife, create a 2- to 3-inch pocket in each breast. Marinate the chicken in the salad dressing in the refrigerator for 2 hours to overnight.

To prepare stuffing, combine olive oil, thyme, and pepper flakes in a saucepan over medium heat. Cook until the spices release their fragrance. Stir in the garlic, basil, artichoke hearts, salt, and pepper. Cook for about 3 minutes. Add the cheese, and blend well. Cook for another minute or two, until the cheese is partially melted. Remove from heat, and cool.

Spoon stuffing into each breast pocket, securing each one using 2 toothpicks.

Preheat the oven to medium high. Cook the chicken for 4 to 5 minutes on each side. Meat should be medium brown, with its juices running clear. Let the chicken rest before removing the toothpicks. ✦

# CB's Grilled Ginger Chicken Tenderloins with Spicy Peanut Sauce

1 pound chicken tenderloins or boneless, skinless chicken thighs, cut into large chunks

3 garlic cloves, minced

2 tablespoons minced fresh ginger

2 teaspoons dark brown sugar

½ teaspoon cumin

½ teaspoon turmeric

½ teaspoon salt

Safflower or peanut oil, as needed

Juice of 1 lime and 1 lemon, as needed

In a large bowl, whisk together all of the ingredients except the chicken. Add to sealable plastic bag. Rinse and pat the chicken dry, and place in bag with marinade. Refrigerate for at least 1 hour and up to 4 hours before grilling.

Preheat grill to medium high. Remove chicken pieces from marinade; place on grill; and discard the contents of bag. Turn the pieces to form sear marks. When the chicken has seared on all sides and has an internal temperature of 165°F (180°F for thighs), it is done. Place on plate, and serve with peanut sauce for dipping. ✤

## PEANUT SAUCE

1 cup creamy peanut butter

½ cup ginger tea, hot

Hot sauce to taste

1 tablespoon garlic powder

1 tablespoon brown sugar

1 tablespoon soy sauce

1 tablespoon peanut oil

In a microwavable bowl, heat the peanut butter until it is runny, not bubbling, about 1 minute. Mix in the ginger tea and the remaining ingredients, reheating as necessary. Pour into container, and cover to keep warm until ready to serve.

# Pacific-Rim Chicken Burgers with Ginger Mayo

¼ cup soy sauce

1 tablespoon hoisin sauce

1 tablespoon honey

1 tablespoon red chili paste

2 pounds ground chicken

2 green onions, thinly sliced

2 jalapeño peppers, minced

4 cloves garlic, minced

1 cup finely chopped cilantro

1 cup finely chopped tarragon leaves

1 egg, lightly beaten

⅔ to 1 cup panko or other

unseasoned bread crumbs

Vegetable oil

8 pineapple rings (fresh or canned)

1 cucumber, peeled and thinly sliced

8 hamburger buns

**2**

*These burgers have a nice, tangy-but-sweet teriyaki flavor, with good caramelization on the outside.*

In a pot over medium heat, warm the soy sauce, hoisin, and honey for 5 minutes, stirring periodically to dissolve the honey and hoisin. Mix in the chili paste, and let the sauce simmer for a few minutes. Remove from heat, and let cool. In a large bowl, combine ground chicken with vegetables and herbs.

After the marinade has cooled, add the egg. Work this mixture gently into the ground chicken. Gently mix in the bread crumbs. Form the mixture into 8 patties by coating your hands (in food-safe gloves) liberally with vegetable oil. (The chicken mixture will be very sticky.)

Rub each patty with a bit of oil on all sides. Chill patties briefly in the refrigerator while you preheat the grill to medium high. Cook about 5 minutes per side, turning when underside has browned and releases easily from the grill. (Be careful that you don't scorch the patties; the sugar in the marinade can burn.)

Cook the pineapple on the grill for roughly 2 minutes per side, or until grill marks appear. To serve, place each burger on a toasted bun, and top with ginger mayo, pineapple, and cucumber slices. ✦

## GINGER MAYONNAISE

½ cup mayonnaise

2 cloves garlic

1- to-2-inch knob of ginger

Juice of 1 lime

¼ teaspoon salt

Put all ingredients into a blender or food processor, and blend until smooth. Refrigerate.

# Barbecued Chicken Thighs au Vin

**6 chicken thighs (about 1½ pounds)**

**1 tablespoon vegetable oil**

**1 tablespoon butter**

**2 tablespoons finely chopped shallots**

**1 clove garlic, minced**

**¼ cup red-currant jelly**

**½ cup red wine**

**¼ cup chicken stock or orange juice**

**1 teaspoon grated orange rind**

**½ teaspoon dry mustard**

**½ teaspoon ground ginger**

Place chicken thighs in a plastic bag or large bowl. In saucepan, heat oil and butter; add shallots and garlic, and cook over medium heat for 5 minutes or until softened. Add jelly, wine, stock, orange rind, mustard, and ginger. Heat only until jelly has melted. Remove from heat; let cool to room temperature.

Pour marinade over chicken. Press air out of bag, and secure with twist tie. Marinate at least 3 hours to overnight in refrigerator. Pour marinade into saucepan; bring to a boil; simmer 5 minutes; reserve.

Place chicken thighs, skin side up, on greased grill heated to medium high. Cook for 20 minutes, with lid closed, brushing occasionally with marinade once most of the fat is rendered from the chicken pieces. Turn each thigh, and cook 10 to 15 minutes longer or until juices run clear when chicken is pierced with fork (180°F). ✤

# CB's V8 Chicken

1 fryer chicken, cut
　　into 8 pieces
1 12-ounce can V8
　　vegetable juice
　　cocktail
½ to 1 cup water
BBQ sauce for glaze

Trim chicken pieces of excess fat and place in a nonreactive bowl or plastic food bag. Add V8 juice and water until meat is covered. Cover bowl or seal bag and refrigerate overnight.

One hour before cooking, remove chicken from marinade; rinse chicken; and pat dry with paper towels. Allow chicken to rest a bit at room temperature.

Preheat half of grill to high. Spray or lightly brush chicken parts with canola oil. Sear over high heat. Because wings and legs tend to cook faster, add them to the grill after starting the breasts and thighs. Use tongs to turn chicken when the skin is seared and releases from grill.

As pieces are seared and begin to brown, place them in a pan away from direct heat. Cover loosely with foil or another pan. Allow chicken to finish cooking in pan until breasts reach an internal temperature of 165°F; thighs, 180°F.

During the final 5 to 10 minutes of indirect cooking, brush on a light coating of BBQ sauce. Serve. ♣

**2**

**Chicken**

*Roasted Asparagus
with Cherry Tomatoes,
Garlic & Olive Oil,
page 69*

*Sometimes the ingredients for great-tasting marinades are already made and ready for the using. By accident, I discovered this idea, and the flavors were very tasty!—CB*

# CB's Easy Smoky Chicken Drumettes Party Platter

**20 chicken wing drumettes**

**2 tablespoons garlic powder**

**1 teaspoon ground ginger**

**1 teaspoon ground mustard**

**1 pinch ground cumin**

**Coarse salt & pepper to taste**

**¼ cup peanut or canola oil**

**¼ cup white wine**

**¼ cup favorite BBQ sauce for dipping**

Rinse and pat dry chicken drumettes, and place them in a large mixing bowl. Add the next five ingredients, and mix thoroughly. Drizzle oil onto drumettes, and mix until chicken is lightly coated with oil and spices.

Preheat grill to high. Place small packet of moist wood chips on grill; when they begin to smoke, reduce heat to medium.

Grill chicken approximately 8 to 10 minutes, turning to prevent burning. Keep lid closed between turns to ensure that the smoke permeates the meat. After drumettes have browned sufficiently, remove them from grill, and place them in the center of a large sheet of aluminum foil. Fold foil around the drumettes, leaving a small opening. Pour wine into opening, and loosely seal foil. Place foil packet with drumettes back onto grill until wine begins to steam. Remove drumettes, and garnish with lettuce, celery, or parsley. Serve with your favorite BBQ sauce. ✤

# Tequila Lime Chicken

4 split boneless, skinless chicken breasts

1 tablespoon fresh minced garlic

½ cup fresh-squeezed lime juice

½ cup gold tequila

1 teaspoon kosher salt

½ teaspoon fresh ground black pepper

1½ teaspoon ancho chili powder

1 tablespoon olive oil

Combine the chicken with remaining ingredients, and marinate for 30 minutes at room temperature. (The acid in the lime juice cooks the chicken, so be careful not to over-marinate.) Heat the grill to medium high, and spray the grates with oil to prevent the chicken from sticking. Grill the chicken over direct heat for about 5 to 6 minutes per side. Cook until nicely browned—it should feel firm and the juices should run clear. The sugars in the tequila and lime juice will blacken the chicken—so move them to a lower heat if it gets out of control. Serve hot off the grill with lime wedges and rice. ✦

**2**

**Chicken**

*Recipe courtesy of Marcia Frankenberg, Minneapolis, MN*

# Cheesy Grilled Chicken Quesadillas

1 large grilled chicken breast, chopped

1 3-ounce package cream cheese, softened

1 cup shredded Monterey Jack cheese

⅓ cup crumbled feta cheese

½ teaspoon dried oregano

4 large flour tortillas

⅓ cup chopped pitted ripe olives

2 tablespoons diced pimento

2 tablespoons thinly sliced green onion

For filling, stir together cream cheese, Monterey Jack, feta, and oregano. Spread ¼ of the filling onto half of each tortilla. Top with chicken, olives, pimento, and green onion. Fold plain side over; press gently to seal edges. Preheat grill to high; then reduce to medium. Place tortillas on grill, flipping once. When cheese has melted (about 5 to 8 minutes), remove and cut into three wedges. Serve immediately. ♣

6–8 Servings • Prep: 10 min. • Grill: 25 min.



# Men in Aprons' Spicy Maple Grilled Wings

**1 package (18–24) chicken wings**
**½ teaspoon each of salt, pepper, and paprika**
**¼ cup pure maple syrup**
**3 tablespoons brown sugar**
**1 tablespoon butter**
**3 tablespoons Thai chili sauce**

Mix together salt, pepper, and paprika; then season wings. Preheat one side of grill to medium, the other side to low. In small saucepan, add syrup, sugar, butter, and chili sauce. Bring to a simmer, whisking briskly. Remove from heat. Grill wings for 2 to 3 minutes per side over medium heat; then transfer them to low heat burner. Continue cooking over this burner, turning occasionally, for about 20 minutes or until skin is nicely browned and crisp. About 2 minutes before removing them from the grill, brush wings with maple glaze. Serve. ✤



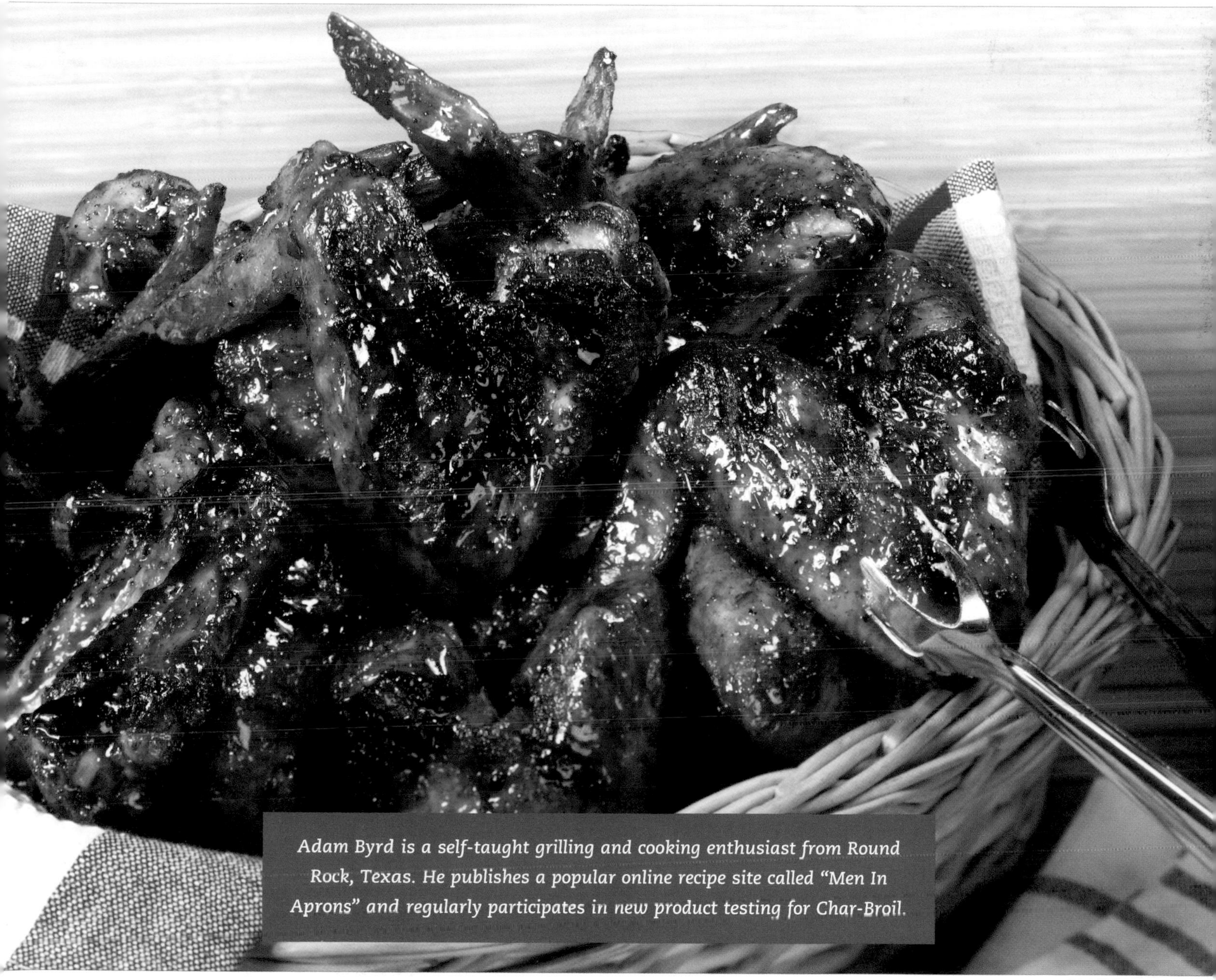

*Adam Byrd is a self-taught grilling and cooking enthusiast from Round Rock, Texas. He publishes a popular online recipe site called "Men In Aprons" and regularly participates in new product testing for Char-Broil.*

# South-of-the-Border Chicken Pizza

1½ cup shredded grilled chicken breast

Store-bought pizza dough

2 cloves garlic, minced

1 cup chopped fresh cilantro

⅓ cup grated fresh Parmesan cheese

6 tablespoons olive oil

Salt and freshly ground black pepper

1¼ cup grated Monterey Jack cheese

2 ripe plum tomatoes, sliced or chopped

½ cup chopped fresh green chilies

Crushed red pepper to taste

Prepare pizza dough, adding one clove minced garlic. Preheat grill to high. In food processor, pulse together cilantro, the rest of the garlic, and Parmesan. Slowly pour in oil until combined and mixture resembles pesto. Add salt and pepper to taste. Reserve for pizza assembly.

When grill is hot, place first pizza crust directly onto oiled grill grates; cook 1 to 1½ minutes until crust becomes somewhat firm. Flip crust over onto baking sheet, with cooked side up. Spread half of pesto mixture on top; then sprinkle with half of Monterey Jack cheese, chicken, tomatoes, green chilies, and crushed red pepper.

Slide pizza off baking sheet back onto grill; placing it so half is over high heat and other half is over medium to low heat. Cook pizza 3 to 4 minutes, rotating frequently to get uniformly brown, crisp crust. Slide pizza onto a serving board, and slice into wedges. Repeat process for second pizza. ✤

# BBQ Orange Chicken

**2½ pounds chicken parts**

**BBQ SAUCE**
¼ **cup vegetable oil**
¼ **cup frozen orange juice concentrate**
½ **cup white wine vinegar**
¼ **cup tomato paste**
**Zest from 1 orange**

Preheat grill to high. In a medium bowl, mix together all sauce ingredients until smooth. Reduce heat to medium on one side; turn off heat on the other side. Place chicken pieces on grill away from heat, skin side down; cook 15 minutes. Turn chicken, and grill for 10 additional minutes. Brush chicken pieces with sauce, and turn occasionally, cooking for additional 10 minutes. ✚

**2**

Chicken

# Do-Ahead Minced BBQ Chicken

**12 chicken-leg quarters**

**1 quart apple cider vinegar**

**⅓ cup low-sodium chicken broth**

**⅓ teaspoon onion salt**

**1 teaspoon coarsely ground fresh pepper**

**2 bay leaves**

**24 sandwich buns**

**1 cup Dijon mustard**

In a large saucepan, mix together the vinegar, chicken broth, onion salt, pepper, and bay leaves. Bring to a boil over high heat. Place the chicken in a bowl, and pour the hot vinegar mixture over it. Cover, and marinate in the refrigerator for at least 2 hours.

Preheat the grill to medium. Place the chicken on the grill, skin side up. Pour 2 cups of the marinade in a small saucepan, and bring to a boil on the grill. Grill the chicken, turning and basting with the boiled marinade every 10 to 15 minutes for about 1 hour or until the internal temperature reaches 165°F.

Remove the chicken from the grill, and let it cool for about 10 minutes. Cut the chicken from the bone; discarding the bones and skin. Place the meat, four quarters at a time, into a food processor and pulse 3 or 4 times until the chicken is coarsely chopped. (Chop with a knife if a processor is not available.) Repeat this with the remaining chicken. (There should be about 9 cups.)

Boil the remaining marinade to reduce it to 1¼ cups; pour over the minced chicken. Serve on toasted buns spread with mustard. Garnish with a dill pickle slice if desired. ✤

# Mastur-K's Chicken on a Stick

**1 medium to large boneless, skinless chicken breast**
**Garlic-pepper mix**
**2 wooden skewers, soaked for at least 30 minutes**

Preheat grill to medium-low. Trim any fat from the chicken. Cut the fillet down the middle into two long strips. (Each piece should look like a chicken tender.) Place tenders in a clean kitchen towel, and pat them dry. Run skewers through both pieces, starting with smaller end. Place the skewers on a placemat or over the sink, and shake on as much garlic pepper mix as desired. Grill skewers for 10 minutes on each side or until chicken is no longer pink in center. (Note: the small end of the chicken should be farther away from the center of the grill so that the larger end can cook evenly.) Serve with rice and vegetables. ✤

*Mastur-K, also known as Kevin W, is a "Sizzle on the Grill" reader and contributor.—CB*

## GARLIC-PEPPER MIX

2 tablespoons black peppercorns
1 tablespoon powdered garlic
1 tablespoon paprika
1 tablespoon Mrs. Dash spice mix (original flavor)

Put all ingredients into a spice or coffee grinder, and process until fine. Put the mixture in a shaker, and use it as you please.

Note: this recipe does not contain salt. You may add a tablespoon or two if desired.

# Grilled Chicken Skewers with Grilled Caesar Salad

**2 4-ounce boneless, skinless chicken breasts**

**1 cup BBQ sauce of your choice**

**2 whole heads romaine lettuce**

**½ cup extra-virgin olive oil**

**½ cup minced shallot**

**½ cup minced fresh garlic**

**Salt and pepper**

**Bamboo skewers soaked in white wine for 1 hour**

**1 prepared log herbed polenta**

**1 cup balsamic vinegar**

**1 jar of your favorite Caesar dressing**

Cut the chicken breasts lengthwise into four equal slices. Place chicken in a plastic bag with the BBQ sauce; seal; and marinate for 1 to 2 hours or overnight. Cut the romaine heads in half lengthwise. Drizzle the olive oil over both sides. Spread the shallot, garlic, salt, and pepper over the cut side of the heads. Set lettuce aside.

Preheat grill to high. Place chicken on skewers, and grill until the meat reaches 165°F. Slice the polenta into ¼-inch slices, and spray with nonstick cooking spray. Grill polenta 5 to 8 minutes on each side to ensure even grill marks. To make the balsamic reduction, place vinegar in a pan over medium heat, and cook until it reduces into syrup. Cool, and reserve. Grill the romaine heads on both sides for 2 to 3 minutes until just wilted. Remove and slice lengthwise; then roughly chop. Toss lettuce very lightly with Caesar dressing. Place a small amount on each plate. Cut the polenta circles in half, and arrange them across the salad. Place the chicken skewers in an "X" over the salad, and drizzle with the balsamic reduction. ✚

*Provided by Erik Lind, 2006 Char-Broil Grilling Team Chef.*

# BBQ Thai Chicken Salad

1 broiler-fryer chicken, about
   3½ pounds

1 tablespoon curry powder

1 14-ounce can unsweetened
   coconut milk, regular or low fat

1 tablespoon lime juice

1 tablespoon fish sauce

3 garlic cloves, minced

¼ cup chopped cilantro leaves

2 tablespoons brown sugar

12 red lettuce leaves, rinsed

1 medium head lettuce, shredded

1 large red bell pepper, sliced

½ cup torn mint leaves

⅓ cup finely chopped peanuts

Rinse the chicken, and pat it dry. Split the chicken in half with a large, sharp knife. In a large bowl, whisk the curry powder into the coconut milk. Blend in the lime juice, fish sauce, garlic, cilantro, and brown sugar. Add the chicken, turning to coat it in the marinade. Cover, and refrigerate 4 hours to overnight.

Preheat the grill to medium. Place the chicken on the grill, skin side down. Turn after about 10 minutes, and continue cooking until the juices run clear or a fork can be inserted into the chicken with ease, about 30 minutes. Cool the chicken slightly; cut it into strips.

Prepare the dressing. Combine all of the ingredients; stir until the sugar dissolves. Arrange the red lettuce leaves on six plates. Combine the shreds of lettuce, bell pepper, and mint; distribute onto lettuce leaves. Scatter the chicken on top. Sprinkle the salad with peanuts; serve with dressing. ✤

**2**

**Chicken**

### SWEET & SOUR CILANTRO DRESSING (makes 1 cup)

⅔ cup rice vinegar

¼ cup sugar

¼ cup minced cilantro

¼ teaspoon salt

½ teaspoon chili paste

⅓ cup safflower or canola oil

# CB's Moroccan-Spice Grilled Chicken & Peaches

2 large boneless chicken breasts

1 15-ounce jar of peaches in natural juice (about 1 cup)

3 tablespoons curry powder

Kosher or sea salt to taste

Cooking oil spray

2 tablespoons olive oil

1 clove garlic, finely chopped

1 tablespoon brown sugar

2 tablespoons balsamic vinegar

3 tablespoons chopped mint or parsley

Strain peaches, and reserve the juice. Rinse the chicken; pat it dry; and season with salt and curry powder. Let chicken reach room temperature, about 15 minutes.

Preheat one side of grill to high; reduce to medium high when grilling. Preheat the other side to medium low. Spray cooking oil on the chicken, and place it on the hot side of the grill for about 4 minutes per side. When both sides have dark grill marks, remove the chicken from the hot side of the grill, and place on the other side to "roast" until done, about 8 to 10 minutes.

In the meantime, warm the oil in a medium pan over medium-low heat. Add the garlic, and sauté until it begins to brown, about 1 to 2 minutes. Add the sugar, vinegar, and peach juice; reduce sauce while chicken cooks.

Using tongs, place the peach slices on hot side of grill to form grill marks. Turn the peaches just once to ensure uniform grill marks. When chicken is cooked to an internal temperature of approximately 150°F, remove and place on a warm plate until the internal temperature is 160° to 170°. Cut chicken into pieces; place the grilled peaches on top; and pour the sauce over both. ✤

# Smoked Chicken "Pâté"

1½ cups smoked chicken thigh meat, bones and skin removed

8 ounces mild goat cheese, softened Camembert (rind removed), or French Neufchâtel*

3 tablespoons finely chopped onion

2 tablespoons favorite dry rub

2 tablespoons mayonnaise

2 teaspoons lemon juice

Hot sauce to taste

Favorite BBQ sauce

*Neufchâtel is a soft, slightly crumbly French cheese that resembles Camembert but with a saltier, sharper taste. American Neufchâtel, very different from the French version, is a lower-fat cream-cheese product.

Grind smoked chicken in a food processor until pieces resemble coarse cornmeal. Using clean hands in food-safe gloves, combine chicken with the next six ingredients in a large bowl.

Transfer mixture to a 2-cup mold that has been coated with cooking spray.

Lightly press mixture into the mold, and cover with wax paper before storing in the refrigerator to set.

At serving time, turn pâté out onto a plate, and sprinkle with additional rub. Drizzle with your favorite BBQ sauce. ✦

**2**

**Chicken**

"Sizzle on the Grill" contributor Larry Gaian says this appetizer is a great way to use leftover smoked chicken thighs.

# Chicken with Goat Cheese & Roasted Red Peppers

4 boneless, skinless chicken breasts

¼ cup plus 2 tablespoons olive oil

2 red bell peppers, roasted

3 ounces fresh, soft goat cheese, sliced into rounds

1 teaspoon chopped onion

1 teaspoon chopped garlic

½ cup white wine

2 teaspoons chopped fresh rosemary

½ stick unsalted butter

Salt and pepper to taste

Sliced almonds, toasted

Preheat the grill to medium high. Wash the chicken, and pat it dry. Brush chicken with 2 tablespoons of olive oil. Grill for 10 minutes or until no longer pink. Remove chicken to a baking dish, and top with the roasted pepper strips and cheese rounds. Bake at 350°F for 5 minutes or just until the cheese is heated through.

Sauté the onion and garlic in ¼ cup olive oil in a heavy skillet over high heat. Add the wine and rosemary. Cook for approximately 3 minutes. Gradually whisk in the butter. Season the mixture with salt and pepper; spoon over the chicken. Top with toasted almonds. ✤

# Grilled Chicken in Olive Oil-Chive Vinaigrette

**4 bone-in chicken breasts**

Dip each piece of chicken in vinaigrette (see right), and coat well. Marinate in refrigerator for a minimum of 4 hours or overnight.

Preheat grill to medium. Place chicken on grill, skin side up. Sprinkle with remaining ¾ teaspoon salt and ¼ teaspoon pepper. Grill, turning and basting with sauce every 10 minutes for about 1 hour or until internal temperature reaches approximately 160°F. ✤

## OLIVE OIL-CHIVE VINAIGRETTE

**6 tablespoons olive oil, divided**
**4 tablespoons red wine vinegar, divided**
**1 teaspoon salt, divided**
**½ teaspoon pepper, divided**
**¼ teaspoon dry mustard**
**1 clove garlic**
**Peel of 1 lemon**
**1 tablespoon chopped chives**

In food processor or blender, place 1 tablespoon of oil, 1 tablespoon of vinegar, and ¼ teaspoon each of salt, pepper, and mustard. Process 15 seconds. While processor is running, add 2 teaspoons olive oil; process 10 seconds. Add remaining 3 tablespoons vinegar, remaining 3 tablespoons oil, garlic, lemon peel, and chopped chives. Process 15 seconds more.

**2**

**Chicken**

# Island Grilled Jerk Chicken

2 pounds boneless, skinless chicken
  breasts
⅓ cup soy sauce
2 tablespoons sesame oil
3 cloves garlic, chopped
3 scallions, chopped
3 tablespoons fresh thyme leaves
1½ teaspoons ground allspice
1½ teaspoons freshly ground pepper
½ teaspoon ground cinnamon
½ teaspoon ground red pepper
16 wooden skewers, soaked in water

## MANGO PAPAYA RELISH

(makes 1½ cups)
1 ripe mango, peeled and diced
1 ripe papaya, peeled and diced
2 scallions, minced
¼ cup minced fresh cilantro
2 teaspoons brown sugar
1 tablespoon lemon juice
Hot sauce to taste

**Combine all ingredients in medium
bowl; cover; and refrigerate at least 1
hour before serving.**

Preheat the grill to medium high. Wash the
chicken, and pat it dry. Cut each chicken
breast in half lengthwise, then into four
strips; place the strips in a plastic storage
bag. Combine the soy sauce and next eight
ingredients in a blender; blend until smooth.
Pour the mixture over the chicken, and
tightly seal the bag. Turn the bag gently to
coat the chicken. Marinate in the refrigerator for at least 1 hour and up to 24 hours.
Thread chicken strips on skewers. Grill on
each side until cooked. Serve with Mango
Papaya Relish. ✿

4–6 Servings • Prep: 15 min. • Marinate: 1 hr.–overnight • Grill: 1½–2 hr.

**59**

# Beer-Can Chicken

**1 whole chicken (4 to 5 pounds)**
**2 teaspoons vegetable oil**
**1 16-ounce can beer**

In a small bowl, combine the rub ingredients. (See below.) Wash the chicken, and pat it dry. Coat the entire chicken with vegetable oil and season it with the rub, inside and out.

Preheat the grill to medium. Pour half of the beer out of the can, and carefully place the half-full can inside the cavity of the chicken. Note: the can will be almost completely covered by the chicken. Transfer the bird to the grill, keeping the can upright. Grill for 1½ to 2 hours or until the internal temperature reaches 180°F in the thickest part of the thigh and the meat is no longer pink. Carefully remove the chicken with the can from the grill using protective mitts. Let the chicken rest for about 10 minutes before lifting it from the can. Discard the beer. Cut the chicken into serving pieces. ♣

## RUB 1
1 teaspoon dry mustard
¼ cup minced onion
1 teaspoon paprika
1 teaspoon kosher salt
4 small cloves garlic, minced
½ teaspoon ground coriander
½ teaspoon ground cumin
½ teaspoon freshly ground black pepper

## RUB 2
3 tablespoons paprika
2 tablespoons sugar
1 tablespoon salt
2 teaspoons coarsely ground black pepper
1 teaspoon onion powder
1 teaspoon garlic powder
1 teaspoon ground red pepper (cayenne)

# Greek Salad Olive-Grilled Chicken

6 split chicken breasts, bone-in

¼ cup olive oil

1 4½-ounce jar prepared black olive tapenade

¼ cup lemon juice

¼ cup chopped fresh oregano

Place the first four ingredients in a resealable plastic bag; add chicken; seal bag; and shake gently to coat chicken with marinade. Refrigerate 4 to 24 hours.

Preheat grill to medium high. Remove chicken from bag, and discard marinade. Arrange chicken on grill. Close lid, and open vents. Cook chicken, turning occasionally to cook all pieces evenly, for about 30 minutes or until a meat thermometer inserted in thickest part of breast registers 165°F. ✤

## GREEK SALAD

1 cup grape tomatoes, halved

12 pitted kalamata olives

6 ounces feta cheese, cubed

½ small red onion, diced

¼ cup extra-virgin olive oil

3 tablespoons lemon juice

1 tablespoon chopped fresh oregano

8 cups mixed greens, preferably spinach, arugula, and romaine

Toss together the first seven ingredients in a bowl. Gently stir in greens. To serve, divide Greek Salad among plates, and top with chicken.

# CB's Grilled Chicken Meatballs

2 pounds ground chicken
1 cup fresh bread crumbs
1 cup Parmesan cheese
2 onions, finely diced
1 medium carrot, finely chopped
1 tablespoon ketchup
1 tablespoon Worcestershire
Your favorite hot sauce to taste
Kosher salt and freshly ground
   pepper to taste
1 egg, beaten
¼ cup roughly chopped cilantro

## SERVE WITH

Marinara sauce
Toasted baguette or sub roll
Shredded mozzarella cheese

The night before, place ground chicken in a colander over a dish, cover, and refrigerate overnight to drain excess moisture.

The following day, combine chicken with remaining ingredients in a large nonreactive bowl using your hands. (Food-safe gloves are recommended.) Form ping-pong-ball-size meatballs, and spray them lightly with canola oil.

Preheat grill to medium high. Use tongs to place meatballs on grill, and turn as searing occurs. If meatballs are seared on all sides and internal temperature has not reached 165°F, use tongs to place meatballs in a disposable aluminum pan; loosely cover with foil; and finish cooking over indirect heat. Close hood.

To make a meatball sub, add your favorite marinara sauce to the aluminum tray while meatballs are finishing. When sauce is warm, serve meatballs on toasted baguette or sub rolls, along with additional sauce. Top with shredded mozzarella cheese. ♣

**2**

Chicken

66

69

71

74

77

79

82

86

89

# 3 Veggies

# Grilled Portobello Mushrooms with Pepperoni & Cheese

4 large Portobello
  mushrooms, stems
  removed, cleaned with
  paper towel
2 tablespoons butter
½ cup shredded mozzarella
½ cup shredded Parmesan
  cheese
Italian seasoning
16 slices pepperoni

*These mushrooms taste like a pepperoni-and-cheese pizza—and you don't have to fling dough.*

Preheat grill to medium. Lightly butter a baking sheet lined with foil. Place mushrooms on baking sheet; add a bit of butter to each; pile shredded cheeses (generously); sprinkle with herbs; and arrange pepperoni on top. Grill until mushrooms are slightly softened and cheese is golden brown, about 10 minutes. Cut in wedges or serve whole. ◊

# Smoky Baby Blue Artichokes

**12 baby artichokes**
**Nonstick cooking**
**  spray**
**Salt and pepper**
**½ cup crumbled**
**  blue cheese**
**Balsamic vinegar**

To prepare the baby artichokes for cooking, snap off the lower petals until you reach the core. Trim each baby artichoke by cutting off the top ½-inch and the bottom stem. Place artichokes in a saucepan filled with water. Bring water to a boil, and parboil artichokes for approximately 3 to 4 minutes. Artichokes are done when a toothpick or knife tip will go into the base of the artichoke easily.

Preheat outdoor grill to medium. Directly spray either mesh grill basket or aluminum foil with nonstick cooking spray. Add artichokes to grill basket or foil, and cook over direct heat for 5 minutes or until artichokes are evenly browned.

Add salt and pepper to taste, and sprinkle blue cheese on top of artichokes. Keep the basket on the grill for one minute or until the blue cheese melts.

Remove the artichokes from the grill, and arrange them on a plate. Drizzle balsamic vinegar over the artichokes, and serve. ◊

**3**

**Veggies**

# CB's Fire-Charred Green Beans with Vinaigrette

1 to 2 pounds fresh green beans, washed, trimmed, and dried
Canola oil
Parmesan cheese, shaved (optional)

*This recipe also works well with sliced zucchini, asparagus, broccoli spears, or steamed artichoke quarters.*

Place beans in a bowl, and coat lightly and evenly with canola oil.

In a nonreactive bowl, mix together anchovy paste, garlic cloves, Dijon-style mustard, Tabasco sauce, Worcestershire sauce, red wine vinegar, and lemon juice, using a whisk or fork.

Gently add olive oil as you continue to stir until all of the ingredients emulsify. Add the salt and pepper as desired. Keep covered and cold until just before serving.

Preheat grill to high. Place the beans at a 90-degree angle to the grates. (Use a grill basket to keep the beans from falling through the grates.) The beans will brown quickly, and the oil can cause flare-ups, so use tongs to move beans often as they cook. When beans are lightly charred, remove to platter, and drizzle with vinaigrette immediately before serving. You can top this dish with shavings of Parmesan cheese after drizzling the dressing on the veggies. ◑

## VINAIGRETTE

1 teaspoon anchovy paste
1 to 2 mashed garlic cloves
1 tablespoon Dijon mustard
½ teaspoon Tabasco sauce
1 teaspoon Worcestershire sauce
2 to 3 tablespoons red wine vinegar
2 tablespoons freshly squeezed lemon juice
Extra-virgin olive oil, as needed
Freshly ground coarse salt and black pepper to taste
Shavings of Parmesan cheese if desired

# CB's Feta-Stuffed Portobellos

6 large Portobello mushroom caps
  (about 3 to 4 inches across)
¼ cup olive oil
¼ cup white balsamic vinegar
Salt and ground black pepper
½ cup crumbled feta cheese
¼ cup chopped sun-dried tomatoes
½ cup baby spinach leaves, washed,
  dried, stems removed
1 teaspoon thyme
1 teaspoon curry powder

*You can vary the size of the mushrooms
to make bite-size hors d'oeuvres or serve
larger ones as a first course.*

Place mushrooms in a large bowl. Add
half of the oil and all of the vinegar,
coating mushrooms on both sides.
Season with salt and pepper, and set
aside.

To the same bowl, add the feta
cheese, tomatoes, and spinach. Add
dry seasonings and remaining oil, and
toss to coat.

Preheat one side of grill to medium high. Place the mushrooms on the
heated side of the grill, and cook for
2 to 3 minutes on both sides. Remove
the mushrooms to a pan on the
unheated part of grill.

Carefully spoon enough stuffing
mixture into each mushroom to fill
each cap. Close the hood, and continue
to cook the mushrooms over indirect
heat. When the cheese begins to melt,
remove mushrooms using tongs, and
place on a serving plate. ◊

# Honey-Grilled Cauliflower

1 cauliflower head,
    rinsed and cut
    into florets
1 cup honey
Salt and pepper
Nonstick cooking
    spray
6 wooden skewers
    (soaked in water)

Preheat grill to medium. In a microwavable bowl filled with 1 inch of water, microwave cauliflower on high for 5 minutes or until the florets are crisp on the outside and tender on the inside.

Arrange four florets on each wooden skewer, and spritz with cooking spray. Place skewers over direct heat; turn until there is an even, light charring on each floret. Remove skewers from the grill.

Brush honey onto the cauliflower; then add salt and pepper to taste. Put back on the grill for another minute or until the honey melts into cauliflower. Remove, and serve immediately. ◊

*Courtesy of www.oceanmist.com*

# Roasted Asparagus with Cherry Tomatoes, Garlic & Olive Oil

2 pounds pencil asparagus, woody ends
   trimmed

2 cups washed and stemmed cherry
   tomatoes

12 garlic cloves, peeled and smashed

¼ cup extra-virgin olive oil

1 teaspoon coarse salt

½ teaspoon freshly ground black pepper

¼ cup fresh lemon juice, reserve lemon
   halves

Preheat the grill to medium high. In a large bowl, combine the asparagus, tomatoes, and garlic. Drizzle with the olive oil, and season with the coarse salt and pepper. Toss to coat; then transfer to a large aluminum baking sheet. Drizzle the lemon juice over the asparagus; add the lemon halves to the pan; and place on the grill. Roast until the asparagus stalks are tender and the tomatoes begin to caramelize, about 20 to 25 minutes. Remove from the grill, and serve hot or at room temperature. ◊

**3**

# CB's Grilled Broccoli & Cauliflower with Toasted Walnuts

**2 large broccoli heads**

**1 large cauliflower head**

**Canola oil spray**

**¼ cup fruit vinegar (such as pear, raspberry, apple, or blueberry)**

**¼ cup chopped and toasted walnuts**

Preheat grill to medium. Trim broccoli and cauliflower into florets about the size of a golf ball. Put them on a large sheet pan, and spray with oil.

Using tongs, move florets to the grill. Turn each one as it sears and chars just a bit. Remove as they finish cooking, 7 to 12 minutes.

Arrange in a mound on a serving platter; drizzle with vinegar; and garnish with walnuts. ◊

# Grilled Potato Planks

1½ **pounds (about 3 large) unpeeled baking**
     **potatoes, cut into ½-inch-thick slices**
3 **tablespoons olive oil**
2 **teaspoons finely chopped fresh rosemary**
1 **garlic clove, minced**
½ **teaspoon salt**

Preheat grill to medium high. Combine oil, rosemary, garlic, and salt in dish. Add potato slices, and turn until well-coated. Grill potatoes for about 8 minutes. Turn, and continue grilling 10 minutes longer or until cooked. Remove from grill, and serve. ◐

*Courtesy of www.christopherranch.com*

# Grilled Eggplant with Cheese

**4 small eggplants**

**Olive oil**

**Salt and pepper**

**½ pound soft goat cheese or feta, crumbled**

**2 teaspoons minced garlic**

**1 teaspoon red pepper flakes**

**1 tablespoon finely chopped fresh basil**

Cut eggplants in half lengthwise. Brush cut edges with olive oil, and season with salt and pepper. In a small bowl, combine cheese, garlic, red pepper flakes, and basil with a pinch of salt, and then refrigerate until ready to use. Preheat the grill to medium. Place eggplant halves on grill over direct heat, skinless side down. Roast until almost soft (2 to 3 minutes). Remove from grill, and cool slightly. Then spread or sprinkle the cheese mixture on the warm eggplant, and serve immediately. ◊

# Cookout Potatoes

Nonstick cooking spray

1 medium onion, halved and thinly sliced

1½ pounds Yukon Gold potatoes, very thinly sliced

1⅓ cups low-fat shredded sharp cheddar cheese

⅓ cup real bacon bits

⅓ cup chopped bell pepper

½ teaspoon garlic salt

Spray a 9 × 9 × 2-inch foil pan liberally with nonstick cooking spray. Layer half the onions, potatoes, cheese, bacon bits, bell pepper, and garlic salt in pan; then layer the other half over the first. Cover the top tightly with foil, and grill over medium heat for 1 hour, rotating pan occasionally to avoid hot spots. ◊

# Creamy Zucchini & Garlic

**2½ tablespoons butter**
**6 garlic cloves, minced**
**6 medium zucchini, grated**
**2½ tablespoons garlic powder**
**1 teaspoon chopped thyme**
**2½ tablespoons sour cream**
**Freshly ground black pepper**

Melt the butter in a heavy-bottom skillet over medium heat. Lower the heat; add the minced garlic; and sauté for about 1 to 2 minutes. (Do not let the garlic burn.) Add the grated zucchini, garlic powder, and thyme.

Cook, stirring frequently until the zucchini is tender. Remove from the heat, and stir in the sour cream. Season with fresh pepper. Serve immediately. ◊

*Courtesy of www.christopherranch.com*

# Spinach-Stuffed Vidalia Onions

**6 medium Vidalia or other sweet onions**

**1 pound fresh spinach**

**2 teaspoons butter, melted**

**¼ cup cream**

**1 teaspoon Worcestershire sauce**

**Salt and freshly ground pepper to taste**

**Dash of cayenne pepper**

**Grated parmesan cheese**

Preheat the grill to medium. Peel the onions, and place them in a steamer rack over simmering water. Steam them until they begin to soften, yet are still firm, about 5 minutes. Remove them from the heat. Wash the spinach, and remove the stems. Pour the water from the onions over the spinach in the colander. Drain the spinach well, squeezing with your hands, and place on a paper towel to drain. Chop the spinach finely. Sauté it in melted butter; add the cream and Worcestershire; and season with salt and pepper.

Hollow the onions, and fill them with the spinach mixture. Sprinkle onions with cayenne pepper and Parmesan cheese. Wrap the stuffed onions in foil, and grill them for about 20 minutes. ◑

**3**

# Garlic-Roasted Sweet Potatoes with Arugula

2 pounds sweet potatoes, peeled and cut into 2-inch pieces

4 garlic cloves, peeled and sliced

2 tablespoons extra-virgin olive oil

½ teaspoon salt

½ teaspoon ground black pepper

2 Bartlett pears, cored and cut into 2-inch pieces

1 5-ounce package arugula

½ teaspoon grated lemon peel

Preheat grill or oven to medium high. In large roasting pan, combine potatoes, garlic, oil, salt, and pepper, and toss to coat well. Roast for 30 minutes, tossing occasionally, until tender and browned. Add pears, and roast another 10 minutes.

Place the arugula in a large bowl. Add the cooked potatoes and pears, and toss until the arugula wilts. Sprinkle with the lemon peel. ◑

Courtesy of
www.christopherranch.com

# Livefire's Holiday Potato Torte

**3 to 4 russet potatoes, scrubbed but not skinned**

**Olive oil**

**Salt and black pepper to taste**

**2 tablespoons chopped fresh rosemary**

**V-slicer or mandolin**

Preheat grill to medium high. Generously butter a well-seasoned 10-inch cast-iron or other heavy skillet. Using a V-slicer or mandolin, thinly slice each potato, placing slices in the skillet as you go to prevent oxidation.

Because you will invert the torte after it is cooked, the bottom layer of potatoes will be the top of the torte, so make sure to arrange the slices in an attractive pattern. As you add each layer, brush it with olive oil, and sprinkle with salt and pepper and about ½ teaspoon of rosemary. When you're finished, you should have about 7 layers of potatoes.

Place skillet on the grill, and cook until the potatoes are sizzling nicely, about 12 to 15 minutes. Using heat-resistant gloves or potholders, remove skillet from the grill, and drain off excess oil. Carefully invert the torte onto a clean plate, and then slide the potatoes, bottom side up, back into the skillet. Return to the grill, and cook, with lid closed, for about 20 to 25 minutes or until potatoes are browned and crispy and inner layers are tender. ◊

**3**

Veggies

# CB's Grilled Fennel

2 large fennel bulbs

2 tablespoons brown sugar

1 teaspoon Worcestershire sauce

2 tablespoons peanut oil or clarified butter

Coarse salt

Remove the green top and fronds from the fennel, and reserve. Quarter each bulb, leaving the root bottoms in place to hold the leaves together during roasting. Whisk together the brown sugar, Worcestershire sauce, and oil. Marinate the pieces in the mixture for 15 to 20 minutes.

Preheat the grill to medium. Using tongs, arrange fennel slices on grates; turn to sear and caramelize all sides, about 3 to 5 minutes. As the edges begin to crisp and char just a bit, remove to a holding pan to finish over indirect heat with the hood closed. The fennel bulbs are cooked when they are fork-tender but not too soft. Serve on a platter with freshly ground salt and a teaspoon or two of finely minced fennel tops. ◊

*This recipe will drive you crazy-go-nuts because it pairs deliciously with just about any grilled meat.—CB*

# Marinated Portobello Mushrooms with Roasted-Pepper Vinaigrette

**1 pound fresh Portobello mushrooms, stems trimmed**
**Olive oil for skillet**

## MARINADE
**4 tablespoons balsamic vinegar**
**6 garlic cloves, minced**
**2 tablespoons chopped fresh thyme leaves**
**⅓ cup olive oil**

In a small bowl, whisk together marinade ingredients. Arrange mushroom caps in a single layer in a nonreactive shallow pan. Pour marinade over mushrooms; cover; and marinate for 1 hour, turning mushrooms several times. In a blender, combine vinaigrette ingredients until smooth. Taste for seasoning.

Heat an oiled grill skillet. Remove mushrooms from marinade; place in pan; and use a food press or a heavy can to press down on them. Sear them about 2 to 3 minutes on each side or until tender. Transfer mushrooms to a cutting board; slice thin; and drizzle with red-pepper vinaigrette. ◊

**3**

*Courtesy of*
*www.christopherranch.com*

## VINAIGRETTE
**1 red pepper, roasted, peeled, seeded, and coarsely chopped**
**1 Poblano chili, roasted, peeled, seeded, and coarsely chopped**
**4 garlic cloves, peeled**
**2 tablespoons red wine vinegar**
**1 lemon, squeezed for juice**
**¼ cup olive oil**
**Coarse salt**
**Freshly ground black pepper**

# Carrots & Raisins Revisited

2 cups plain non- or low-fat yogurt

1 tablespoon packed brown sugar

¼ teaspoon grated orange peel

2 tablespoons orange juice

¼ teaspoon ground nutmeg or cardamom

¼ teaspoon Tabasco sauce

6 to 7 medium carrots, peeled and
　　shredded coarsely

3 cups dark raisins

3 tablespoons chopped cashews,
　　almonds, or pecans

Line a medium-size strainer with a double layer of rinsed cheesecloth or a triple layer of white paper towels. Place the strainer over a large bowl, and spoon yogurt into it. Let yogurt drain for 1½ hours; then scrape it into a medium-size bowl. Discard strained liquid.

Stir brown sugar, orange peel and juice, nutmeg, and Tabasco sauce into the yogurt until smooth. Mix in carrots and raisins, and toss to coat. Cover, and chill 20 to 30 minutes. Just before serving, sprinkle with chopped nuts. ◑

# Savory Corn Pudding

2 tablespoons butter, melted

4 medium shallots, finely chopped

1 small cubano or jalapeño pepper, seeded and finely chopped

1 ripe tomato, chopped

8 ears fresh corn

¾ cup whole milk

½ cup heavy cream or milk

Salt and pepper to taste

1 to 2 teaspoons red pepper flakes (optional)

2 tablespoons fine yellow cornmeal (optional)

2 to 3 tablespoons fresh lime juice

1 cup slivered fresh basil

1 tablespoon olive oil

1 tablespoon minced fresh chives (optional)

1 to 2 teaspoons finely chopped fresh oregano (optional)

In 3-quart saucepan over medium-low heat, sauté shallots in butter 6 minutes or until translucent. Add pepper and tomato; cook another 2 to 3 minutes.

Using a sharp paring knife, scrape kernels from the corncobs into a bowl; transfer corn and juices to the saucepan, and stir another 2 to 3 minutes. Add milk, ¼ cup at a time, stirring until absorbed; then pour in the cream, and season with salt, pepper, and pepper flakes if desired. If necessary, thicken mixture with cornmeal, 1 tablespoon at a time, until it is puddinglike. Add the lime juice, basil, olive oil, and optional herbs. ◑

*Courtesy of cookbook author and food blogger Cathy Erway*

**3**

Veggies

# CB's EZ Grilled Asparagus Soup

2–3 garlic cloves, unpeeled

Olive oil

2–4 pounds asparagus, washed and trimmed of tough ends

1 large yellow or sweet onion, chopped

Freshly ground pepper and kosher salt

Chicken stock or vegetable broth (1 cup per serving)

1–2 tablespoons of flour or cornstarch

1 tablespoons unsalted butter

¼ cup light cream or whole milk

*Instead of cooking asparagus and onions in a stockpot, I prefer to grill them. The charring adds a wonderfully smoky taste.—CB*

Preheat grill to medium high. Oil unpeeled garlic cloves; wrap in aluminum foil; and place on heating rack of grill for about 30 minutes. When garlic is soft, remove from heat. Peel; mash garlic in a small bowl; and set aside.

Lightly coat asparagus and onions with oil and season with pepper and salt. Place on grill. Using long tongs, turn vegetables often to create grill marks, but be careful not to burn them. Remove when done.

In blender, puree grilled asparagus and onions, gradually adding ½ cup of chicken stock to help liquefy. Place puree into a large stockpot, and simmer for about 25 minutes, adding more stock if necessary. Stir in flour, butter, cream, and roasted garlic. Simmer for about an hour to allow flavors to meld. If desired, strain soup through a sieve for a smoother texture. Ladle into individual bowls or cups. Garnish with grilled asparagus tips. ◊

# Grilled Spuds with Dipping Sauce

**4 large potatoes, peels on**
**Chives, minced**
**Bacon, cooked and crumbled**

### DIPPING SAUCE

**¾ cup olive oil**
**3 tablespoons fresh lemon juice**
**1 large garlic clove, minced**
**1 tablespoon grated Parmesan**
**1 teaspoon Worcestershire sauce**
**2 tablespoons minced chives**
**Salt and freshly ground pepper**

*This dipping sauce is also great on salads.*

Preheat oven to 400°F. Wash potatoes; rub with oil; then prick with fork. Bake 1 hour directly on oven rack, and remove from oven when tender. Cut potatoes in half lengthwise, and let cool. Scoop out center, leaving shell about ¼ inch thick. Reserve pulp for another use.

Preheat grill to medium. Whisk together dipping sauce ingredients in a small bowl. Brush potato skins lightly with dipping sauce, and grill for 3 to 4½ minutes per side, until crispy. Arrange skins on platter, and sprinkle with chives and bacon. Serve warm with dipping sauce. ◊

**3**

# Georgia "Caviar"

2 cans whole-kernel corn, drained

1 can finely diced tomatoes, drained

2 cans black-eyed peas, drained and rinsed

1 10-ounce bottle Italian dressing

2 cans diced tomatoes with green chilies

1 large red onion, finely diced

1 each red, green, and yellow bell pepper, finely diced

2 teaspoons salt

3 tablespoons finely chopped cilantro

Tabasco to taste

Combine all ingredients; let set a minimum of 4 hours. (Overnight refrigeration is best.) Serve with your favorite dipping chips. Leftovers will keep for at least one week in refrigerator. ◑

# Stuffed Mushrooms on the Grill

24 large mushrooms, cleaned and stems removed

2 tablespoons butter

2 teaspoons minced onion

¾ cup shredded sharp cheese

⅓ cup bacon bits

⅓ cup bread crumbs

2 tablespoons chopped parsley

1 to 2 tablespoons sherry (optional)

Preheat grill to medium. Mix stuffing ingredients together; stuff mushroom with mixture.

Cut six squares of heavy-duty aluminum foil. Wrap four mushrooms in each square of foil; seal; and place on grill. Grill 12 to 15 minutes without turning packets. Serve while hot. ◊

**3**

Veggies

# Grilled Corn with Sun-Dried Tomato Pesto

**4 ears of corn in husks**
**½ cup sun-dried tomatoes**
**2 tablespoons whole pine nuts**
**¼ cup olive oil**
**1 teaspoon chopped garlic**
**Salt and pepper to taste**

Soak the corn in water for 45 minutes to 1 hour. Place the remaining ingredients in a blender; puree until smooth.

Preheat grill to medium. Remove the corn from the water. Peel back the husks, leaving them attached at the stem. Grill the corn for 8 to 10 minutes, turning often. Remove from the grill, and spread the corn with the sun-dried pesto. Serve immediately. ◊

# Uncle Jim's Time-Tested Grilled Corn

**4 ears corn, still in husk**
**Olive oil for brushing**
**Garlic or onion, chopped**
  **and caramelized**
**Fresh herbs**
**Nutmeg**
**Sea salt**
**Black pepper**

Pull back on each corn husk, but do not remove it. Remove and discard corn silk; then soak the cobs in a pot of cold water for 15 minutes. Preheat the grill to medium. Remove the corn from the water, and brush the kernels with olive oil. Spread corn with the caramelized garlic or onion, fresh herbs, nutmeg, sea salt, and black pepper. Tie the husks back in place with twine. Place the prepared ears of corn over direct heat on the grill, turning every few minutes to create grill marks. Finish the corn with indirect heat on the top shelf of the grill with the cover closed. Allow the corn to roast for another 15 minutes. ◊

**3**

**Veggies**

# Eggplant Roll-Ups

**1 medium eggplant, sliced lengthwise into ¼-inch-thick slices**

**Salt and pepper to taste**

**1 red pepper**

**1 green pepper**

**1 red onion**

**½ cup mayonnaise**

**1 tablespoon cranberry sauce**

**2 large pitas**

Place the eggplant on a flat baking sheet; sprinkle both sides with salt and pepper. Let this stand 10 to 15 minutes.

Cut each pepper in half, and trim away the ribs and seeds. Cut the onion into rings. Preheat the grill to medium-high.

Place the eggplant, peppers, and onions on the grill, and cook 4 to 5 minutes for peppers and onions, 6 to 8 minutes for eggplant.

Grill the pitas for approximately 2 to 3 minutes until toasted; remove them from the grill.

Spread the cranberry sauce mixed with mayonnaise onto each pita; add the vegetables; and roll up pitas. ◊

# Grilled Zucchini Parmesan

**3 zucchini or yellow squash, sliced**
**2 tomatoes, diced**
**½ teaspoon oregano**
**Salt and pepper to taste**
**3 tablespoons melted butter**
**3 tablespoons grated Parmesan cheese**

Preheat the grill to medium-high. Place the zucchini and tomatoes on six squares of aluminum foil. Sprinkle the oregano, salt, and pepper on top of each. Top with butter. Seal the foil lightly, and grill for 20 to 25 minutes, turning every 10 minutes. Remove the foiled vegetables from the grill; unwrap them; and sprinkle them with Parmesan cheese. ◊

3

Veggies

# Chinese-Style Vegetables

**1 head baby bok choy**
**1 head napa cabbage**
**⅛ cup olive oil**
**⅛ cup chicken broth**

Preheat the grill to medium. Separate the bok choy and cabbage leaves, and rinse them thoroughly; then dry the leaves with paper towels. Mix the olive oil and chicken broth, and sprinkle the mixture onto the vegetable leaves. Put vegetables into a grill wok or basket, and grill, basting with the oil and broth mixture, until the leaves are just tender. ◑

# Carrots with Snap

32 baby carrots or 8 regular carrots, cut
   into 2-inch pieces
½ jalapeño pepper, seeded and chopped
¼ teaspoon unsalted butter
Salt and black pepper to taste

Place eight baby carrots each on four pieces of heavy-duty foil. Add the chopped pepper and butter to each; then add salt and pepper to taste. Fold up the edges of each piece of foil to create a tight seal to form packets. Grill the packets over medium heat, turning once, for 20 to 25 minutes. ◊

# CB's Grilled Artichokes

**2 large, fresh artichokes**
**2 tablespoons olive oil**
**1 tablespoon kosher salt or sea salt**
**Freshly ground black pepper**

Using kitchen shears, trim the tips of the artichoke leaves about ½ inch down. Rinse artichokes thoroughly with water; then slice them in half to expose the heart and "choke."

Steam the artichokes in a pot on the range until tender, about 10 to 15 minutes. Remove from pot, and chill in an ice-water bath until cool to touch. (Hint: use previously cooked artichokes stored overnight in a cooler.)

Preheat the grill to low. Using a teaspoon, carve away the choke, making sure to leave the heart. You can cut these halves once more to create quarters if you prefer. Drizzle the artichokes with olive oil, and season them with salt and pepper. Grill cut side down—checking or turning side-to-side every few minutes—until grill marks begin to show. Remove, and serve artichokes as a side dish or appetizer.

Season ready-made mayonnaise with tarragon, parsley, and lemon zest for dipping. ◊

*A CB-and-son recipe from "Sizzle on Grill" for Father's Day 2006*

# Grilled Green Beans with Walnuts

¾ **pound green beans, trimmed**

**2 teaspoons olive oil**

**¼ cup toasted and finely chopped walnuts**

**2 teaspoons walnut oil**

**2 teaspoons fresh lemon juice**

**Freshly ground pepper**

Toss the beans with oil, and grill them for 5 to 8 minutes in an oiled grill basket until tender. Remove beans, and toss with walnuts, walnut oil, and lemon juice. Season the beans with pepper, and serve immediately.

# Garlic-Grilled Portobellos

**4 Portobello mushrooms, about 1 pound**

**⅓ cup extra-virgin olive oil**

**3 tablespoons lemon juice**

**2 cloves garlic, peeled and minced**

**Salt and pepper to taste**

**2 tablespoons minced fresh parsley**

Preheat the grill to medium-high. Brush any dirt or grit off the mushrooms with a damp paper towel. Remove the stems. Combine the oil, lemon juice, and garlic in a bowl. Brush the caps on both sides with the garlic oil; sprinkle salt and pepper on both sides, and let them stand for 15 minutes, stem side up. Place the caps on a well-oiled grill, stem side up; grill them for 3 to 4 minutes. Turn the caps over, and grill them for another 3 to 4 minutes or until easily pierced with a knife. Do not burn or overcook them; the centers should be tender and moist. Transfer the caps to a platter, and cut them into thick slices. Garnish with parsley before serving. ◑

# Indian-Spice Grilled Cauliflower

**4 tablespoons butter**
**¼ teaspoon cinnamon**
**¼ teaspoon dried coriander**
**½ teaspoon grated fresh ginger**
**⅛ teaspoon crushed saffron threads (optional)**
**¼ teaspoons ground cardamom**
**1 tablespoon minced garlic**
**1 head cauliflower, cut into florets**

In a skillet, cook the butter over medium heat until golden brown. Combine the cinnamon, coriander, ginger, saffron, cardamom, and garlic; stir this mixture into the butter. Add the cauliflower, stirring to coat the florets with sauce, and cook for 3 to 4 minutes, stirring occasionally. Transfer the cauliflower florets to a grill basket, saving any remaining sauce for basting. Grill the vegetables over high heat, basting and turning them frequently. Cook for 5 minutes or until they are crunchy-tender. Be careful not to overcook. Serve. ◊

**3**

**Veggies**

# Double-Grilled Stuffed Potatoes

6 large baking potatoes
Stuffing mixture

### STUFFING MIXTURE

1 16-ounce carton sour cream
1½ cups shredded cheddar cheese,
    divided
1 stick butter, softened
2 teaspoons salt
Pepper to taste
1 pound barbecue pork butt, finely chopped
1 each large red, yellow, and green bell
    pepper, finely diced

Place the hot potatoes in a large mixing
bowl. Add the sour cream, ¾ cup of cheese,
and butter, blending well. Stir in the salt,
pepper, and finely chopped pork.

*Serve these hearty potatoes as a main dish with salad or
as a side dish.*

Preheat the grill to high. Wash the potatoes; pierce
them with a fork; and wrap them in aluminum foil.
Grill for 45 minutes or until the potatoes test done.
Allow them to cool slightly.

Unwrap the potatoes. Cut each in half lengthwise.
Carefully scoop the potato out of each half to within
¼ inch of skin, reserving the skins. Add potatoes to
stuffing mixture. Spoon the mixture into the reserved
potato skins. Sprinkle the remaining cheese and finely diced bell peppers over the potatoes. Return them
to the grill, and cook them over medium heat until
the cheese melts.

Note: potatoes can be prepared ahead of time and
returned to the grill or oven just before serving. ◍

# Grilled Red Potatoes & Green Beans with Pesto

1 pound fresh green beans, rinsed and trimmed

2 cups water

12 red potatoes (about 1½ pounds)

Nonstick vegetable oil spray

2½ cups basil leaves

¼ cup chopped Italian parsley

2 tablespoons olive oil

⅓ cup vegetable broth

2 large garlic cloves, peeled and halved

¼ cup pine nuts

¼ cup grated Parmesan cheese

Steam beans in microwave or steamer basket on stovetop until almost tender, about 8 minutes. Transfer beans to bowl of ice water to stop cooking. Drain beans, and cut them in half.

Preheat grill. Thread three red potatoes onto each of four skewers. Spray the potatoes and grill with oil. Place the skewers on the grill. Turning as needed, grill 20 to 30 minutes or until potatoes are tender. Remove potatoes from grill; set aside. When cool enough to handle, remove potatoes from skewers, and cut each potato in half. Set aside.

To make pesto, combine basil, parsley, olive oil, broth, garlic, pine nuts, and Parmesan in a food processor or blender. Blend until ingredients resemble a sauce. Transfer to a bowl.

While grill is still hot, place wire basket on grill; lightly oil basket; and then add potatoes and beans. Place basket on grill, and heat, tossing frequently, 4 to 5 minutes. Remove from grill, and divide mixture among four plates. Serve with pesto. ◊

**3**

Veggies

# Spicy Grilled Fries

1 tablespoon paprika

1 teaspoon freshly ground
  black pepper

1 teaspoon kosher salt

½ teaspoon chili powder

Pinch of cayenne (optional)

4 large russet or baking
  potatoes, scrubbed but
  not peeled

Olive oil

Preheat the grill to medium low. Combine the first five ingredients in a small bowl. Cut the potatoes in half lengthwise; then slice each half into long wedges that are about ½ inch thick in the middle. Place the potatoes in a large plastic storage bag, and pour the oil on top. Shake well to coat; then sprinkle the potatoes generously with the spice mixture, and shake again until they are well coated. Place the potatoes directly on the grate, and grill for 30 to 35 minutes, turning every 5 to 7 minutes. Dab them lightly with additional oil as needed. The potatoes are ready when crisp and golden brown outside and soft in the middle. ◐

# Mushroom-Stuffed Potatoes

4 large baking potatoes

Salt and freshly ground black pepper to taste

4 tablespoons butter

1 tablespoon minced green onions

1 clove garlic, minced

8 ounces fresh mushrooms, sliced

¼ cup heavy cream

1 tablespoon minced fresh chives

1 tablespoon minced fresh parsley

¼ cup grated Swiss or Gouda Cheese

Preheat the grill to high. Wash the potatoes; pierce them with a fork; and wrap them in aluminum foil. Grill for 45 minutes or until the potatoes test done. Allow them to cool slightly. Unwrap the potatoes and slice the top off each one, cutting horizontally. Carefully scoop out the potato pulp to within ¼ inch of skin, reserving the skins. Season the potato shell with salt and pepper. Place the hot potato pulp in a large mixing bowl.

In a medium saucepan, melt the butter, and sauté the onions and garlic for 1 minute over medium-high heat. Add the mushrooms, and sauté until tender. Add the cream; cook and stir the mixture over medium heat until well blended. Remove from the heat, and add the chives and parsley. Pour the mushroom sauce onto the potato pulp, and fold them together. Spoon the stuffing into the potato shells, and top with cheese. Place the shells on a baking sheet, and heat them in the oven at 350°F for 20 minutes or until potatoes are warm and the cheese is brown and bubbling. ◊

**3**

Veggies

# Smoked Gouda Sweet Potatoes with Praline-Pecan Crumble

**4 tablespoons butter, divided**

**2½ pounds sweet potatoes, peeled and cut into ¾-inch cubes**

**½ teaspoon salt**

**1 teaspoon Creole seasoning**

**1 cup shredded smoked Gouda**

**1½ cups cranberry juice**

**½ cup dark brown sugar**

**3 tablespoon flour**

**½ cup chopped pecans**

**⅛ teaspoon nutmeg**

Preheat the oven to 375°F. Spread 1 tablespoon of butter over the bottom and sides of a 9 × 12-inch baking dish.

Layer the cubed sweet potatoes in the baking dish, and toss them with the salt, Creole seasoning, and smoked Gouda. Pour cranberry juice over the mixture. Cover the dish, and bake for 30 minutes.

In the meantime, melt the remaining butter in a saucepan over low heat. Stir in the brown sugar, flour, pecans, and nutmeg. Mix well, and set it aside until the potatoes and cheese finish baking.

Remove the casserole from the oven, and spoon the pecan mixture over top. Continue baking, uncovered, for an additional 30 minutes. ◐

*This sweet and savory recipe, submitted by Judy Armstrong of Prairieville, Louisiana, has a short list of special holiday ingredients, is quick to assemble, and complements the flavors of fried, grilled, or smoked poultry.*

# CB's Honey-Butter Sweet Potatoes

**6 medium sweet potatoes**
**¼ cup honey**
**¼ cup unsalted butter**

Preheat the grill to medium. Cut the sweet potatoes into ½-inch slices, and place them on grill. Mix the honey into the softened butter. After the sweet potato slices have grilled for 8 to 10 minutes, spread them with the honey-butter mixture, and turn them. Grill the slices for 8 minutes more; then turn them, and spread on more honey butter. Continue grilling until the honey butter is bubbling and the sweet potato slices are tender. Serve hot or warm. ◊

**3**

**Veggies**

# Grilled-Corn & Black Bean Salad

2 ears corn, grilled

1 cup cooked black beans, drained and rinsed if canned

1 small red bell pepper, peeled, cored, and seeded

3 tablespoons fresh lemon juice

1 garlic clove, minced

2 tablespoons chopped fresh cilantro

2 teaspoons chopped fresh tarragon

Salt and freshly ground pepper to taste

3 tablespoons olive oil

Using a sharp knife, cut the corn kernels from the cob. In a large bowl, combine the black beans, corn, and bell pepper. In a small bowl, whisk together the lemon juice, garlic, herbs, salt, and pepper. Add the olive oil, blending well. Pour the dressing mixture over the corn and black bean salad, tossing well. Serve at room temperature or chilled. ◐

# Grilled Endive with Blue Cheese

**6 heads endive**

**4½ tablespoons olive oil**

**Salt and pepper to taste**

**¾ cup crumbled blue cheese**

**2 tablespoons balsamic vinegar**

**2 tablespoons chopped fresh parsley**

Heat the grill to medium-high, and preheat the broiler. Cut each endive lengthwise into two sections, and place in a single layer on a baking sheet. Brush the endive with 4 tablespoons of oil; then sprinkle with salt and pepper. Grill until crisp-tender, about 1 minute per side. Return endive to the baking sheet. Sprinkle with cheese. Broil until the cheese melts and bubbles, about 2 minutes. Transfer the endive-cheese combination to a platter. Drizzle with ½ tablespoon oil and the balsamic vinegar. Top with parsley. Serve immediately. ◊

**3**

# Salt-Grilled Potatoes

**2 medium russet, white, or yellow-flesh potatoes, or 3 or 4 small red potatoes**

**Coarse salt**

Preheat grill to medium high. Poke several holes in each potato to vent steam. Cover bottom of an aluminum loaf pan with salt. Place potatoes in pan, and cover completely with salt. Grill over direct heat with grill lid closed for 40 minutes or until potatoes are done. Use oven mitts to remove pan from grill. Remove potatoes from pan, and brush off excess salt. ◊

# Mixed-Mushroom Pita Pizza

5 button mushrooms, sliced

2 shiitake mushrooms, sliced

2 oyster mushrooms, sliced

1 large portabello mushroom, sliced

2 tablespoons diced red onion

½ each red and green bell pepper, julienned

2 cloves garlic, crushed

¼ cup white wine

¼ cup chicken broth

2 pocketless pita breads

1 cup tomato sauce

1 cup shredded mixed cheese

Preheat grill to medium-low. Place one or two sheets of aluminum foil over grill grates. Add mushrooms, onion, and peppers to medium saucepan with garlic, wine, and chicken stock; sauté for 5 to 7 minutes. Drain liquid. Cover pita with tomato sauce. Add mushroom mixture; then sprinkle with cheese. Place on aluminum foil over medium-low grill until cheese melts. ◐

**3**

114

122

126

127

# 4 Sides

# Asian Super Slaw

6 tablespoons rice vinegar

6 tablespoons vegetable oil

5 tablespoons creamy peanut butter

3 tablespoons soy sauce

3 tablespoons golden brown sugar, packed

2 tablespoons minced fresh ginger

1½ tablespoons minced garlic

5 cups thinly sliced green cabbage

2 cups thinly sliced red cabbage

2 large red or yellow bell peppers, cut into matchstick-size strips

2 medium carrots, peeled and cut into matchstick-size strips

8 large scallions, cut into matchstick-size strips

½ cup chopped fresh cilantro

Salt and freshly ground black pepper, to taste

*This colorful, Asian-inspired salad is great with grilled chicken.*

Whisk together the first seven ingredients in a small bowl to blend. Cover, and let chill. (The dressing can be made 1 day ahead.) Let the dressing stand at room temperature for 30 minutes before continuing.

Combine the remaining ingredients in a large bowl. Add the dressing, and toss to coat. Season the salad with salt and pepper, and serve. ❖

# Mexican Potato Salad

3 medium fresh green chilies

2 pounds red potatoes, skin on, cut into wedges

6 medium tomatillos, husked and cut into ½-inch pieces

1¼ cups chopped scallions

¼ cup fresh chopped cilantro

1 cup sour cream

3 tablespoons fresh lime juice

2 teaspoons ground cumin

Salt and freshly ground pepper to taste

*Perfect with Southwestern-style chicken.*

Preheat grill to high. Grill the chilies until blackened on all sides. Enclose chilies in a paper bag, and let them rest for 10 minutes. Peel, seed, and chop the chilies; transfer them to a large bowl.

Steam the potatoes until just tender, about 10 minutes. Cool, and combine them with the chilies. Mix in the tomatillos, scallions, and cilantro.

Whisk together the sour cream, lime juice, and cumin in a small bowl. Pour the mixture over the potatoes and chilies; then gently toss just to coat potatoes. Season with salt and pepper. Cover, and refrigerate for 4 to 6 hours to blend the flavors. Let salad stand at room temperature for 30 minutes before serving. ❖

**4**

Sides

*Tomatillos are green, tomato-like vegetables with thin, paper-like husks. They are available at Latin American markets and some supermarkets. If you can't find them, substitute green or yellow tomatoes.*

# Layered Corn-Bread Salad

### CORN BREAD

1 tablespoon vegetable
   oil

3 cups buttermilk

2 eggs

2 cups yellow cornmeal

1 teaspoon baking soda

1 teaspoon baking
   powder

1 teaspoon salt

½ cup chopped jalapeño
   peppers

Preheat the oven to 450°F. Coat the bottom and sides of a 10-inch iron skillet with vegetable oil, and heat it in the oven. In a medium bowl, combine the buttermilk and eggs; stir. Add the cornmeal, baking soda, baking powder, salt, and jalapeño peppers, continuing to stir briskly. Pour the batter into the hot skillet. Bake for 20 minutes or until lightly browned. ❖

### DRESSING

1 package ranch-style dressing mix

8 ounces sour cream

1 cup mayonnaise

1 pan corn bread (from recipe),
   crumbled

2 16-ounce cans pinto beans,
   drained

3 cups shredded cheddar cheese

3 large tomatoes, chopped

½ cup chopped green bell pepper

½ cup chopped green onions

½ cup chopped chili peppers

1½ cups bacon pieces

1 15-ounce can corn, drained

Combine the dressing mix, sour cream, and mayonnaise; set aside. Place half of the crumbled corn bread in the bottom of a large serving bowl. Top with 1 can of pinto beans. Follow this with half of the cheese, tomatoes, bell peppers, green onions, chili peppers, bacon, corn, and dressing mixture. Repeat this process, ending with the dressing mixture. Cover and chill mixture for at least 2 hours before serving.

6 Servings • Prep: 1 hr. • Chill: 1 hr.–overnight • Grill: 10 min.

**111**

# Grilled Polenta

3 cups water

1 teaspoon salt

2 tablespoons unsalted butter

¾ cup polenta or coarse-ground yellow cornmeal

¾ cup freshly grated Parmesan cheese

¼ teaspoons cayenne pepper

Olive oil

*Great with grilled chicken breasts.*

Combine the water, salt, and butter in a saucepan, and bring to a boil. Gradually add the polenta, whisking constantly to avoid lumps. Reduce heat, and continue cooking, stirring constantly, until mixture is very thick, 10 to 15 minutes. Remove the pan from the heat, and stir in Parmesan cheese and cayenne pepper.

Line a 9-inch pie plate with plastic wrap, letting it extend over the edges. Spread the polenta evenly over plastic wrap, and smooth the top. Cover tightly with plastic wrap, and chill until firm, at least 1 hour.

Preheat the grill to medium. Invert the pie plate to allow molded polenta to be removed. Peel off the plastic wrap. Cut the polenta into six wedges. Brush each wedge lightly on both sides with oil. Arrange the polenta wedges on the cooking grate. Grill, turning 2 or 3 times, until golden, about 10 minutes. ❖

**4**

Sides

# Becky's Barley Casserole

½ cup Marsala wine

2 cups chicken broth

1 cup pearl barley

1 tablespoon butter

1 medium onion, chopped

1 4-ounce can whole button mushrooms, drained

¼ teaspoon dried rosemary

⅛ teaspoon freshly ground black pepper

1 tablespoon chopped fresh parsley

Preheat the oven to 350°F. Combine the wine and broth in a 2-quart microwave- and oven-safe casserole dish. Microwave on high until the mixture boils, about 4 to 5 minutes. Stir in the barley, butter, onion, mushrooms, rosemary, and pepper. Cover the dish tightly, and bake for approximately 1 hour or until the liquid is absorbed and the barley is tender. Fluff the barley with a fork, and garnish it with chopped parsley. Serve warm. ❖

*Rebecca Anderson, a "Sizzle on the Grill" reader from Melissa, Texas, makes this fuss-free dish during the holiday season.—CB*

# Original Oklahoma BBQ Beans

2 pounds dry pinto beans

1 tablespoon salt

1 whole onion, peeled and split (secure with 2 wooden toothpicks to hold together)

2 large cloves garlic, with wooden toothpick inserted into each

¼ pound salt pork, slab bacon, or smoked jaw

⅓ cup shortening

2 cups finely minced onions

½ cup all-purpose flour

2 cups tomato juice (or ¾ cup tomato sauce, or ⅓ cup tomato paste diluted to make 2 cups)

Salt and pepper to taste

¼ cup firmly packed brown sugar

¼ cup molasses

Hot pepper sauce to taste

Soak the beans overnight in 2 quarts water. Discard the water, and rinse the beans thoroughly. Transfer to a large pot and fill with water to 1 inch above surface of beans. Add salt, whole onion, garlic cloves, and salt pork. Cover, and simmer over medium heat until beans are tender, not mushy. Remove from heat.

In saucepan, heat shortening and minced onion over high heat. Sauté until onions are translucent. Add flour, and stir until mixture turns golden. Remove from heat, and add tomato juice, salt, and pepper. Stir until lump-free. Discard whole onion and garlic from beans. Ladle some beans into sauce; then stir sauce back into bean pot. Stir in brown sugar and molasses. Remove salt pork and discard, or cut into small pieces about size of beans, and stir in pork. Add the hot pepper sauce. Bring the mixture to a boil, stirring; then remove from the heat.

Let beans stand for at least 1 hour before serving. ❖

**4**

Sides

# George JV's Ranch Beans

1 pound ground beef

1 package dry onion soup mix

½ cup water

1 cup ketchup

2 tablespoons prepared
   mustard

2 tablespoons vinegar

1 can (11-ounce) pork and beans

1 can (28-ounce) baked beans

1 small can lima beans
   (optional)

Preheat the oven to 400°F. Brown the ground beef in a large skillet. Stir in the remaining ingredients, and pour the mixture into a 2-quart casserole dish. Bake for 30 minutes. ❖

# Buttery Bourbon Scallions

24 scallions, washed, trimmed, and peeled

⅓ cup bourbon

1 tablespoon butter

1 teaspoon brown sugar

Salt and freshly ground pepper to taste

Place the scallions in a large bowl. Combine the bourbon, butter, and sugar in a saucepan. Place over medium heat, and cook just long enough to melt the butter and dissolve the sugar. Pour the mixture over the scallions; toss well.

Cut two squares of aluminum foil, stacking them to make them double the thickness. Transfer the scallions and sauce onto the foil, making sure to get all remaining sauce out of the bowl. Wrap the foil around the scallions, leaving sides high enough to contain the sauce, and seal them at the top.

Preheat the grill. Place the foiled scallions on the grill, away from direct heat. Close the lid, and grill for 30 to 40 minutes, stirring several times to make sure the scallions don't char. ❖

*Great with chicken.*

4

Sides

# Marian's Homemade Tomato Pickle

2 pounds tomatoes

1 green pepper

3 red peppers

1 large eggplant

1 pound onions, peeled and
   finely chopped

4 large cloves garlic, crushed

14 ounces sugar

½ pint malt vinegar

1 tablespoon salt

2 tablespoons paprika

*Marian is a regular reader of "Sizzle on Grill." She prepares this mild relish each year for her friends and family to enjoy. Her advice: "It takes a while to make this pickle, so I make enough for 12 months of use."—CB*

Blanch the tomatoes by placing them in boiling water for a few seconds; drain; then place them in ice water. The skins will come off easily. Chop the tomatoes; then seed, clean, and chop the peppers and eggplant. Put vegetables in a large, heavy pan with the onions and garlic; bring it to a boil. Cover the pan, and simmer for about 1 hour, stirring occasionally, until the veggies are tender.

Add the sugar, vinegar, salt, and paprika to the pot, and bring to a boil over medium heat, stirring until the sugar has dissolved. Continue to cook the mixture for 20 minutes until it achieves the consistency of chutney. (Keep constant watch at the end of the cooking time to make sure the pickle does not burn on the bottom of the pan.)

Spoon the pickle into sterilized canning jars, and top them with a waxed-paper cutout; then place a lid on the jars. Leave them to cool overnight, and retighten the lid on each jar in the morning. Place the jars in a dark, cool place for at least 4 weeks to mature the flavors. ❖

# Stuffed Tomatoes on the Grill

6 large tomatoes

Ketchup to taste

1½ cups herb-seasoned stuffing

½ cup grated Romano cheese

2 tablespoons chopped scallion

Dash pepper

2 tablespoons butter, melted

Preheat the grill to medium-high. Slice the top portion from each tomato; discard. Scoop out the pulp from each tomato. Chop and drain the pulp. Turn the tomato shells upside down on a paper towel to drain them.

In a bowl, combine the chopped tomato pulp, ketchup to taste, stuffing mix, cheese, scallion, pepper, and butter. Lightly salt the tomato shells; fill them with stuffing mixture. Wrap the bottom of each tomato in aluminum foil. Grill for about 30 minutes. ❖

**4**

Sides

# Peg's Magic Beans

1 pound maple-cured bacon

1 large white onion, finely chopped

1 pound 80-percent-lean ground beef

1 can (15½ ounces) dark-red kidney beans

1 can (15½ ounces) white cannellini beans or great northern beans

1 can (15½ ounces) black-eyed peas or navy beans

1 can (8 ounces) baked beans

1 can (15½ ounces) medium to hot chili beans

1 bottle (12 ounces) chili sauce

1 cup brown sugar

6 ounces apple cider vinegar

1 tablespoon garlic powder

1 tablespoon chili powder

½ tablespoon paprika

Hot sauce to taste

The night before cooking beans, fry the maple-cured bacon in a large skillet or frying pan until crisp. Remove the bacon; crumble when cool. Drain fat from skillet, reserving about 1 teaspoon. Cook onion and ground beef in the skillet with the reserved bacon fat until meat is browned. Drain off the fat, and transfer the onions, cooked ground beef, and bacon to the cooking sleeve of a 5-quart slow cooker.

Drain and rinse all of the beans except the chili and baked beans. Then add all of the beans, chili sauce, brown sugar, vinegar, and spices to the rest of the ingredients. Stir well. Cover with plastic wrap, and store in the refrigerator overnight.

The next day, transfer the cooking sleeve with the beans and meat to the slow cooker set on low for a minimum of 4 hours. Serve warm. ❖

*From "Sizzle on the Grill." I can testify to the great taste of these beans!—CB*

# Aunt Sylvia's Buttermilk Coleslaw

5 to 6 cups tightly packed
   Savoy or other cabbage
1 large carrot, julienned or
   grated
1 cup julienned jicama or
   Granny Smith apple
1 cup diced or thinly sliced
   sweet onion
Coarse salt
2 garlic cloves, mashed
⅓ cup buttermilk
¼ cup extra-virgin olive
   oil
2 tablespoons fresh lemon
   juice
¼ teaspoon celery seeds
Freshly ground black pepper

Combine the cabbage, carrot,
jicama, and onion in a colander,
and lightly season with salt. Put
the colander in a large bowl; set
a plate on top of the vegetables;
and place a can of soup or beans
on top of the plate for extra
weight. Allow the vegetables
to drain for 1 to 2 hours in the
refrigerator. Then turn the mixture onto a sheet pan lined with
paper towels; pat dry; and transfer to a dry bowl.

   In a small bowl, mix the
mashed garlic, buttermilk, olive
oil, lemon juice, celery seeds,
and pepper. Toss the slaw with
the dressing, and season with
salt, pepper, and lemon juice to
taste. May be kept in the refrigerator for up to a day before
serving. ❖

*This version of slaw
was something my Aunt Sylvia
would make for summer backyard
cookouts. It's great as a side.—CB*

# Greek Potato Salad with Sun-Dried Tomatoes

1 pound (3 medium) potatoes, cut into ¼-inch slices

1 cup (1½ ounces) sun-dried tomatoes, halved lengthwise

1 cup sliced seedless cucumber

½ cup sliced red onion

1 cup crumbled feta cheese

½ cup Greek olives or pitted black olives

In 2-quart saucepan over medium heat, cover potatoes with 2 inches of water. Bring to a boil; reduce heat; and cook until tender, about 12 minutes. Drain, and set aside. Meanwhile, put the sliced sun-dried tomatoes in a small bowl, and pour boiling water over them; set aside 10 minutes.

Whisk together all of the dressing ingredients in a large bowl. Thoroughly drain tomatoes, and pat dry with paper towels. Add potatoes, tomatoes, and cucumbers to the bowl, and toss with the dressing. Transfer the potato salad to a serving plate. Garnish with onion, cheese, and olives. ❖

**LEMON DRESSING**

¼ cup olive oil

¼ cup water

2½ tablespoons lemon juice

1 large garlic clove, pressed

1 tablespoon chopped fresh oregano, or 1 teaspoon dried oregano leaves

1 teaspoon salt

½ teaspoon pepper

# Black-eyed-Pea Salad

## BEANS

1 tablespoon extra-virgin olive oil

1 medium onion, chopped

3 or 4 garlic cloves, minced

1 pound black-eyed peas, rinsed and drained

6 cups water

1 bay leaf

Salt to taste

## DRESSING AND SALAD

¼ cup red wine vinegar or sherry vinegar

1 garlic clove, minced

Salt and pepper, freshly ground, to taste

1 to 2 teaspoons cumin, lightly toasted and ground

1 teaspoon Dijon mustard

½ cup broth from the beans

⅓ cup extra-virgin olive oil

1 large red bell pepper, diced

½ cup chopped cilantro

Heat 1 tablespoon olive oil in a large, heavy soup pot over medium heat; add onion; and cook until tender, about 5 minutes. Add half the garlic. Once it is fragrant, about 30 seconds to 1 minute, add the black-eyed peas and the water. Simmer, skimming off any foam from the surface. Add the bay leaf and salt, to taste (1 to 2 teaspoons). Reduce the heat; cover; and simmer 30 minutes. Taste and adjust salt, if needed. Add the remaining garlic; cover; and simmer until the beans are tender but intact. Remove from the heat; drain over a bowl. Transfer the beans to a large salad bowl.

In a small bowl, whisk together vinegar, garlic, salt, pepper, cumin, and mustard; add ½ cup of the bean broth and the olive oil; blend with whisk. Taste and adjust seasonings. Toss dressing with the warm beans. Stir in the red pepper and cilantro. Serve warm or at room temperature. ❖

**4**

Sides

# CB's Smoky, Cheesy Cornbread

1½ cups cornmeal

1 cup all-purpose flour

1 teaspooon baking soda

½ teaspooon salt

3 tablespoons sugar

¼ cup vegetable oil

2 large eggs

1 cup buttermilk

4 ounces smoked cheese, such
   as smoked Gouda or smoked
   blue cheese

Preheat grill to medium. Lightly grease a small cast-iron skillet or a 9 x 5 baking pan.

Whisk together first five ingredients; then add oil, eggs, and buttermilk; use spatula to mix until just combined. Ladle batter evenly into pan. Crumble cheese on top, and let rest for 15 minutes; then bake in grill over indirect heat for 30 to 35 minutes. (Check doneness by inserting a toothpick in the center; it should come out clean.) Remove, and cool for a few minutes. Run a butter knife around the edge; place cooling rack on top of skillet or pan; and flip. Cool for 30 minutes before slicing. ❖

# CB's Cucumber Salad

2 to 4 medium-size cucumbers (7 to 10 inches each), thoroughly washed and dried

Salt

## GINGER DRESSING

3 tablespoons Japanese rice vinegar or apple cider vinegar

1 tablespoon coarse salt

1 tablespoon freshly squeezed lemon juice

1 tablespoon sugar

1 tablespoon peeled and finely grated ginger

¼ teaspoon grated lemon rind

Score the skin of the cucumbers with a fork, or peel off skin in strips. Slice cucumbers into very thin rounds; place sliced cucumbers in a colander; sprinkle with salt; and toss to mix thoroughly. Let cucumbers rest for 15 to 20 minutes. Meanwhile, make the dressing by mixing together the vinegar, salt, lemon juice, sugar, ginger, and lemon rind in a nonmetallic bowl. Set aside.

Once the salted cucumbers have drained, remove them from the colander, and place them into a large, clean dishtowel or cheesecloth; gently blot excess moisture. Then add cucumbers to the bowl, and toss with the dressing. Chill before serving. ❖

**4**

Sides

# Better-than-Mom's Mac & Cheese

1 box (16 ounces) corkscrew or
   mini penne pasta
¼ cup butter or margarine
¼ cup all-purpose flour
4 cups milk
¾ teaspoon salt
1½ teaspoons Tabasco sauce
1 cup shredded Gruyère cheese
1 cup shredded sharp cheddar cheese

## BREAD-CRUMB TOPPING
⅓ cup butter or margarine
½ cup dried seasoned bread crumbs
½ teaspoon Tabasco sauce

Prepare pasta as directed on box. Drain; set aside.

Meanwhile, melt butter in 3-quart saucepan over medium heat. Stir in flour until blended and smooth. Gradually whisk in milk, salt, and Tabasco sauce. Cook until thickened and smooth, stirring often. Add cheese to sauce, and stir until melted. In large bowl, toss sauce with cooked pasta. Spoon mixture into an ungreased 2-quart baking dish.

Preheat oven to 375°F. To prepare bread-crumb topping, melt butter or magarine in a small skillet over medium heat. Stir in bread crumbs and Tabasco sauce; blend well. Top pasta mixture with prepared bread crumbs and cheese. Bake 20 minutes until crumbs are toasted and casserole is completely heated. ❖

# Cranberry-Pecan Rice Pilaf

**2 tablespoons butter or margarine**

**1 cup uncooked rice**

**1 can (14½ ounces) chicken broth**

**1 cup grated Parmesan cheese**

**½ cup dried cranberries**

**½ cup chopped pecans, toasted***

**¼ cup sliced green onions**

**Salt and freshly ground black pepper, to taste**

*To toast pecans, spread nuts on small baking sheet. Bake 5 to 8 minutes at 350°F, or until golden brown, stirring frequently.*

Melt butter in 2-quart saucepan over medium heat. Add rice; cook, stirring, 2 to 3 minutes. Add broth, and heat to boiling, stirring once or twice. Reduce heat; cover; and simmer 15 minutes or until liquid is absorbed.

Remove from heat. Stir in cheese, cranberries, pecans, and onions. Season to taste with salt and pepper. ❖

**4**

**Sides**

126

8 Servings • Prep: 10 min. • Cook: 3½ min. • Chill: up to 8 hr.

# Harvest Slaw with Sweet Potatoes

12 ounces sweet
   potatoes, cubed
12 ounces packaged
   broccoli slaw
½ cup dried cranberries
   or raisins
1 green apple, diced

½ cup sliced almonds
1 teaspoon ground
   cinnamon
¼ teaspoon garlic salt
¼ teaspoon black pepper
½ cup ranch dressing

Place sweet potatoes in a micro-wave-safe dish or plastic food bag. Microwave for 3½ minutes; let cool for 5 minutes. In a large bowl, combine the potatoes with the rest of the ingredients. Toss with ranch dressing. Chill up to 8 hours before serving. ❖

# Grilled Stuffed Tomatoes Caprese

6 plum tomatoes, stemmed, tops cut off, and insides scooped out

Small bocconcini or other fresh mozzarella, cut into 6 1-inch cubes

**DRY INGREDIENTS**

½ cup Italian bread crumbs

⅓ cup freshly grated Parmesan or Romano cheese, plus extra for topping

8 fresh basil leaves, chopped, with 6 additional leaves for garnish

**WET INGREDIENTS**

1 tablespoon balsamic vinegar

2 tablespoons extra-virgin olive oil

1 teaspoon sugar

Dash hot sauce

Clean and scoop out the plum tomatoes; then insert 1 bocconcini or piece of mozzarella into each.

Separately combine the dry and wet ingredients, and then mix them together well. Stuff the tomatoes with the mixture, mounding it slightly. Top each tomato with extra grated Parmesan, and place them into a greased muffin pan.

Preheat your grill for indirect cooking, with one side hot and one side warm. Grill the tomatoes over the hot side for about 4 minutes, turning them often. Then move them to the warm side; close the grill lid; and let them cook an additional 5 minutes, turning pan occasionally, until all the cheese is melted.

Top each tomato with a small basil stem and leaf, and serve hot as a side dish or appetizer. ❖

**4**

Sides

*Thanks to www.girlsonagrill.com for their contribution as guest chefs and writers.*

# cific Rice

...ng grain rice
1 cup sliced green onions
¾ cup salted cashews
¼ cup seasoned rice vinegar
1 tablespoon sesame seeds, toasted*

Cook rice according to package directions; there should be about 3 cups of cooked rice. While it's still hot, combine the rice with the onions, cashews, vinegar, and sesame seeds. Toss well. ❖

*To toast sesame seeds, spread them on a small baking sheet. Bake at 350°F for 5 to 8 minutes, stirring occasionally, or until golden brown.

# Miss Allison's One-Beer Skillet Bread

3 cups self-rising flour

¼ cup sugar

Pinch salt

1 can beer

1 egg, beaten

### OPTIONAL ADDITIONS

Sliced onions, corn, bacon
  bits, bell pepper, jalapeño,
  or chopped herbs

Preheat grill to medium low. Mix flour, sugar, salt, and beer, and lightly knead into a dough. Pour dough into a well-seasoned cast-iron skillet, or add a bit of bacon grease to the bottom and sides of a pan. Brush the top of the dough with the beaten egg; then top with the onions, corn, or other additions.

Place skillet on grill over indirect heat. Close lid. After about 50 minutes, move the skillet over direct heat, and continue cooking for 10 minutes.

Skillet bread is done when toothpick inserted in the center comes out clean. Flip bread over onto a cooling rack. Serve in wedges. ❖

**4**

# Grilled Bread & Tomatoes

¼ **cup butter, melted**

1 **tablespoon chopped garlic**

½ **loaf day-old French bread, cut into 1-inch slices**

5 **tomatoes, seeded and cut into chunks**

½ **red onion, finely chopped**

¼ **cup extra-virgin olive oil**

¼ **cup balsamic vinegar**

**Salt and pepper to taste**

1 **tablespoon coarsely chopped Italian parsley**

1 **tablespoon coarsely chopped fresh basil leaves**

Preheat the grill to medium-high. Melt the butter in a small saucepan; then add the chopped garlic. Brush the garlic butter on both sides of the bread slices. Grill the bread over medium-high heat until lightly browned, 3 to 4 minutes for each side.

Cut the grilled bread slices into quarters, and place them on a plate. Top with the chopped tomato and red onion. Drizzle the olive oil and balsamic vinegar over the top. Sprinkle with salt, pepper, parsley, and basil. Let stand about 30 minutes to allow the bread slices to absorb the liquids. Serve at room temperature. ❖

# Deviled Potato Bites

12 to 15 small potatoes
Water
Pinch of coarse salt
2 teaspoons mustard
2 tablespoons mayonnaise
½ cup chopped fresh dill

Wash each potato, and cut the top off. Cut larger potatoes in half. (See photo.) Bring a large pot of water to a boil, and add salt. Carefully drop potatoes into the pot, and boil for 10 to 20 minutes, depending on size, until easily pierced with a fork.

Scoop the center of each cooked potato into a bowl. Add mustard and mayonnaise; mix well; and spoon into the potato halves. Top with dill. ❖

**4**

"As I looked at these pretty little red and blue-purple potatoes, I decided to do something kind of like a deviled egg that showed off their colors. I separated the blue and red potato fillings and used a couple of whole red potatoes (no skin) to make a little more. These are perfect appetizers for a party, or a great snack or side dish. They're also a great substitute for potato salad at a BBQ."— Diana Johnson, dianasaurdishes.com

136

139

140

142

# 5 Desserts

# CB's Grilled Pears with Honey & Thyme

**Canola oil spray**

**1 ripe pear, cored and sliced into eighths**

**1 tablespoon honey**

**1 teaspoon chopped fresh thyme**

*This easy dessert will cook quickly, especially if the grill is already hot.*

Preheat the grill to medium. Spray the pear slices with canola oil, and grill, turning as needed, until they are slightly soft and grill marks appear. Arrange four slices in a fan shape on each plate. Drizzle with honey, and sprinkle with thyme. Serve as is or with a dollop of ice cream or whipped cream if desired. ∾

# Rice Pudding with Dark Chocolate Sauce

**5 ounces uncooked white rice**

**2 pints milk**

**7 tablespoons butter**

**½ teaspoon vanilla extract**

**⅓ cup sugar**

**¼ teaspoon nutmeg**

## FOR THE SAUCE:

**5 ounces dark chocolate chips**

**2 tablespoons water**

**1 tablespoon butter**

In a medium saucepan, combine the rice, milk, butter, vanilla, nutmeg, and sugar. Bring the mixture to a gentle simmer over medium-high heat. Reduce the heat to low; cover; and simmer until the mixture is thick and pudding-like, about 10 minutes. Be careful not to scorch the bottom.

In a separate saucepan, heat the chocolate, water, and butter over low heat, and stir until the mixture is smooth and shiny, about 5 minutes. Add 2 to 3 heaping spoonfuls of chocolate sauce to each serving of the rice pudding. ∽

*This dessert is courtesy of Adam Byrd, who says, "This is the most decadent thing I have made to date."*

**5**

**Desserts**

# Grilled Pineapple with Rum & Coconut

**1 ripe pineapple, peeled
and cut crosswise
into 6 slices**

**2 to 3 tablespoons
dark rum**

**1 teaspoon granulated
sugar**

**1 cup whipped cream**

**¼ cup shredded coconut,
toasted**

*With or without a scoop of ice cream, this grilled dessert will be a huge hit at your
next outdoor party.*

Pour the rum and sugar into a bowl with the pineapple. Mix to coat the slices
evenly; cover with plastic wrap; and let it rest for 3 to 5 minutes. Preheat the
grill to medium high.

   Lightly sear the pineapple directly over the heat for about 10 minutes, using
tongs to turn once. Make sure the fruit does not become overly charred.

   Remove pineapple from grill, and top with whipped cream and coconut.
You can also add a heaping scoop of your favorite ice cream if desired. &#8766;

# Bacon Chocolate-Chip Cookies

1 cup all-purpose flour

1 cup bread flour

½ teaspoon salt

½ teaspoon baking soda

¾ cup unsalted butter, melted

1½ cups turbinado sugar or light-brown sugar

1 egg

1 egg yolk

⅛ teaspoon cinnamon

1 tablespoon vanilla extract

2 cups semisweet chocolate chips or chunks

¼ pound bacon, fried crisp and crumbled

Preheat the grill to 325°F, and set up for indirect cooking. Grease cookie sheets, or line them with parchment paper or baking mats. Sift the flour, salt, and baking soda; set aside.

Using a mixer, combine the sugar and butter; add eggs, cinnamon, and vanilla; and mix until creamy. Blend in the sifted ingredients; then fold in the chocolate chips and crumbled bacon using a spatula or a wooden spoon.

Drop ¼-cup-size dough balls onto a cookie sheet, spaced about 3 inches apart, and bake for 9 minutes; then turn and bake for an additional 7 to 9 minutes. Let the cookies cool slightly on the sheet for a few minutes before moving them to a rack to finish cooling. ✐

# Grilled Peaches with Raspberry Puree

**4 medium peaches, sliced
in half and pitted**

**3 teaspoons honey**

**2 tablespoons brown
sugar**

**1 cup raspberries**

**¼ cup orange juice**

**¼ cup butter**

Preheat grill to medium. Combine butter, 1 teaspoon of honey, and brown sugar in a medium sauce pan. Bring to a low boil. Place the peaches in the sauce; let simmer 4 to 5 minutes.

Remove the peaches from the sauce; place on grill, cut side down. Turn peaches over when grill marks appear, about 2 to 3 minutes. Continue grilling 2 to 3 minutes more.

Remove peaches from the grill. In a blender, puree orange juice, raspberries, and remaining 2 teaspoons of honey to a saucelike consistency. Place the peaches on a plate, and drizzle them with the raspberry mixture. ↝

# Tim Barr's Smoked Pears with Berry Compote

4 ripe pears
Berry
   compote
1 cup
   chocolate,
   melted
1 cup
   chopped
   hazelnuts,
   toasted

**5**

Desserts

### BERRY COMPOTE

¼ cup pomegranate, blackberry, or apple juice

4 cups mixed berries, such as raspberries, blackberries, and blueberries, fresh or frozen

⅓ to ½ cup of turbinado sugar

¼ cup honey

½ teaspoon ground cloves

½ teaspoon ground nutmeg

1½ teaspoons vanilla extract

Place the juice in a medium saucepan over medium-low heat. Add the berries, and let them slowly break down for 30 to 40 minutes. (Allow frozen berries to thaw completely, and drain them well before cooking.) Do not let berries boil. When berries have cooked down, add the sugar, honey, cloves, and nutmeg; and continue cooking for another 30 to 40 minutes over low to medium heat, barely simmering, until the mixture is thick. Take the pan off the heat, and add the vanilla. Stir well, and allow the mixture to cool for at least an hour, preferably until it reaches room temperature, before putting it in the refrigerator overnight to set.

The next day, preheat the grill to medium. Halve the pears and spoon out the centers. Add compote to each. Save the remaining compote to use as wanted. Cook the pears in a foil pan or on a piece of foil in the smoker or grill at medium heat for 20 to 30 minutes, just until the pears start to soften. In the meantime, chop and toast the hazelnuts, and also melt the chocolate over the double boiler or carefully in microwave. Once the pears are done, spoon the chocolate over the compote and pears; top them with toasted hazelnuts; and serve warm. ➛

*Although his position with the U.S. Coast Guard takes him all over the country, Tim Barr still finds time to concoct great recipes like this one for the grill. —CB*

# Grilled Pound Cake with Cherry-Nut Ice Cream

¾ cup dried cherries

1 cup boiling water

5 tablespoons brandy

1½ pints vanilla ice cream, softened slightly

4 tablespoons coarsely chopped semisweet chocolate

⅓ cup coarsely chopped nuts (pecans, walnuts, or almonds)

1 loaf pound cake

¼ cup unsalted butter

Place the cherries in a medium bowl. Pour 1 cup of boiling water over them. Let them stand until softened, about 10 minutes. Drain and pat them dry. Mix the cherries and 1 tablespoon of brandy in a small bowl. Place the ice cream in a large bowl. Mix in the cherries, chocolate, and nuts. Cover the ice cream mixture; freeze until firm, about 2 hours.

Preheat the grill to medium. Cut the pound cake into ½-inch slices. Brush both sides of each slice with melted butter. Grill the slices until lightly toasted, about 30 seconds per side.

Place two cake slices on each of eight dessert plates. Place a scoop of ice cream on top. Drizzle 1½ teaspoons of brandy over each serving. ∾

# Frozen Strawberry Pie

## CRUST

**4 tablespoons sugar**

**14 chocolate graham crackers, crushed**

**1 tablespoon butter, melted**

## FILLING

**12 ounces white-chocolate chips**

**6 egg whites**

**1 pint heavy cream, sweetened**

**1 teaspoon vanilla**

**1 pound fresh strawberries**

**1 cup strawberry glaze or jelly**

Combine sugar with chocolate graham crackers; add butter; press into a springform pan; and bake at 375°F for 6 to 7 minutes. Set aside to cool.

Melt white-chocolate chips in a double boiler, and let cool lightly. Beat egg whites until stiff, and then set aside. Whip cream with vanilla; set aside.

Wash the strawberries; pat dry with paper towels; and chop, reserving a few for garnish. Place into a bowl with the strawberry jelly. Fold the egg whites into the whipped cream; then fold in the strawberry mixture, followed by the white chocolate. Pour the filling into the pie crust, and freeze.

Remove the pie from the freezer about 15 minutes before serving to soften slightly. Garnish with the reserved strawberries.

# CB's Nutella & Marshmallow Quesadillas

4 soft flour tortillas

8 tablespoons Nutella or thick chocolate sauce

8 tablespoons marshmallow creme

2 tablespoons butter, melted (½ tablespoon per tortilla)

2 teaspoons cinnamon

2 teaspoons sugar

Preheat grill to low. Warm, but do not brown, the tortillas; then lay them flat on a work surface. Spread 2 tablespoons of Nutella and 2 tablespoons of marshmallow creme on top of each one; fold them in half; and return them to the grill. Cover with an inverted aluminum pan for quick heating.

When the Nutella and marshmallow are sufficiently heated and oozing slightly out of the tortillas, remove the quesadillas from the grill, and quickly brush them with melted butter. Finish with a sprinkling of cinnamon and sugar. Serve warm. ⌇

# Grilled Pineapple with Yogurt & Walnuts

½ cup orange juice

½ cup mango juice or other fruit nectar

2 tablespoons maple syrup

1 tablespoon cornstarch

4 slices fresh pineapple, about
   ¾-inch-thick

Oil for grilling

1 cup of vanilla or other flavored yogurt

1 cup shelled walnuts

Preheat grill to medium low. Combine first four ingredients in a saucepan and bring to a boil; continue cooking for 3 to 5 minutes until sauce thickens. Brush pineapple slices with oil, and grill for 6 to 8 minutes, turning once. Remove pineapple from grill, and place in bowls. Top pineapple with yogurt, and sprinkle with walnuts. Serve immediately. ∾

**5**

# Mississippi River Pie

1½ cups crumbled chocolate sandwich cookies

2 tablespoons unsalted butter, melted

1½ quarts coffee ice cream

1 cup chunky-style peanut butter

8 ounces semisweet chocolate chips

2 cups heavy cream

1½ tablespoons confectioners' sugar

Preheat the oven to 350°F. Combine the crumbled cookies together with the melted butter in a medium bowl. Press the crumb mixture over the bottom of a 10-inch springform pan. Bake for about 14 to 16 minutes or until firm. Chill the crust in the freezer for about 15 minutes.

Place the ice cream in a large bowl, and allow it to soften slightly. Stir in the peanut butter; then press the mixture into the chilled crust. Quickly return the ice cream to the freezer for about 2 hours.

Just before serving, remove ice cream from the freezer. Next, make the chocolate sauce by slowly melting the chocolate chips and ½ cup of cream in a microwave or over a double boiler. Whip the remaining 1½ cups of cream until soft peaks form. Sprinkle the cream with sugar, and continue whipping until stiff peaks form. Release the pie from the springform pan, and cut it into wedges. To serve, pour warm chocolate sauce over each wedge, and top with whipped cream. ✍

# Banana Bliss

2 ripe bananas, unpeeled
2 cups miniature
   marshmallows
2 cups semisweet
   chocolate chips
Brown sugar

Leaving the peel on, slit the bananas lengthwise, but not all the way through the peel. Put half of the marshmallows and chocolate chips in the slit of each banana. Lightly sprinkle brown sugar on top of each banana. Wrap each banana tightly in foil, making sure to seal ends. Place on a medium-hot grill, seam side up, for about 7 minutes. Carefully remove bananas from grill; place in serving dish; unwrap; and serve hot. ❧

**5**

**Desserts**

# CB's Cranberry-Apple Skillet Crisp

### FILLING

1 pound cranberries, fresh or
   frozen

1¼ cups granulated sugar

3 tablespoons grated orange peel

¼ cup water

5 pounds apples (combination of
   Granny Smith, Honey Crisp, or
other firm baking apple),
peeled, cored, and cut into
½-inch pieces

1 cup raisins

3 tablespoons instant tapioca

1 teaspoon vanilla extract

1 teaspoon nutmeg

1 teaspoon pumpkin pie spice

### TOPPING

¾ cup all-purpose flour

½ cup packed light-brown sugar

½ cup granulated sugar

1 teaspoon ground cinnamon

12 tablespoons (1½ sticks)
   unsalted butter, cut into
   ½-inch pieces and chilled

¾ cup old-fashioned oats

Simmer the cranberries, ¾ cup of the sugar, grated orange peel, and water in an ovenproof pot over medium-high heat. When the mixture has a jamlike consistency, remove to a bowl.

Add the apple slices, remaining sugar, and raisins to the pot to cook. When the apples have softened, about 5 to 10 minutes, combine them in the bowl with the cranberries. Blend in the remaining filling ingredients.

**FOR THE TOPPING:** In a food processor, blend the flour, sugars, cinnamon, and butter. Remove to a medium-size bowl. Pour oats into the food processor, and pulse until they are the texture of coarse crumbs.

Combine with the flour mixture, and using your fingers, pinch the topping to make peanut-size clumps. Chill for 1 hour.

Preheat grill to medium-high. Pour filling into a greased cast-iron skillet; scatter topping over it.

Bake over indirect heat, hood closed, for about 30 minutes. (Rotate the pan after 15 minutes for even baking.) The crisp is done when the juices are bubbling and the topping is brown. Serve hot with whipped cream or vanilla ice cream. ⌒

# Peanut Butter & Marshmallow Finger Sandwiches

½ cup heavy cream

2 ounces semisweet chocolate, chopped

1 pound cake

½ cup peanut butter

⅓ cup marshmallow creme

2 tablespoons unsalted butter, melted

In a microwave-safe bowl, heat cream and chocolate on high for 30 seconds; stir; heat for about another 30 seconds, making sure that cream does not boil. Let the mixture stand until the chocolate is melted, about 5 minutes, stirring occasionally.

Preheat the grill to medium high. Using a knife, trim off the top of the cake so that it is even on all sides. Cut the cake in half horizontally. Spread the peanut butter on one half and the marshmallow on the other. Put the two halves together, and brush the top and bottom with butter.

Grill, turning once, until both sides are warm and golden, about 3 to 5 minutes. Transfer to a platter, and cut the cake into thin finger sandwiches. Serve with the chocolate dipping sauce. ⌒

150

155

163

169

# 6 Marinades, Sauces & Rubs

# Maître d' Butter

Yield: 2 cups
Prep: 10 min.
Refrigerate: 1 hr. or overnight
Use with: vegetables

1 pound (4 sticks) unsalted butter, softened
3 tablespoons lemon juice (about 1 lemon)
¼ cup chopped Italian (flat-leaf) parsley, or
   other herbs or spices as desired

In a large bowl, mash the butter. Add lemon juice and parsley and, using a wooden spoon, blend.

Spread a 1-foot-square piece of plastic wrap across a work surface, and scoop the butter mixture on top. Gently wrap the plastic film around the butter, forming a cylinder. Tie off the ends of the wrap with string or a twist tie. Chill or freeze until needed.

*Maître d' Butter is simply softened butter with seasonings, which is rolled and chilled. You can serve it in slices on top of vegetables. Experiment by combining your favorite herbs and spices.*

# CB's Basic Brine Recipe

**Yield:** 4 cups brine
**Prep time:** 10 min.
**Brining Time:** 4 hr.–overnight
**Use for:** smoked poultry

¼ **cup kosher salt**
¼ **cup packed brown sugar**
**4 cups hot water**

In a medium bowl, combine the salt, sugar, and water. Whisk vigorously until salt and sugar have dissolved. Allow the mixture to cool. Pour brine over meat, poultry, or fish. Marinate for several hours or overnight in the refrigerator. Before smoking, rinse the meat's surface, and pat it dry.

Note: the meat should be fully submerged in the brine; make more brine by converting the recipe as needed.

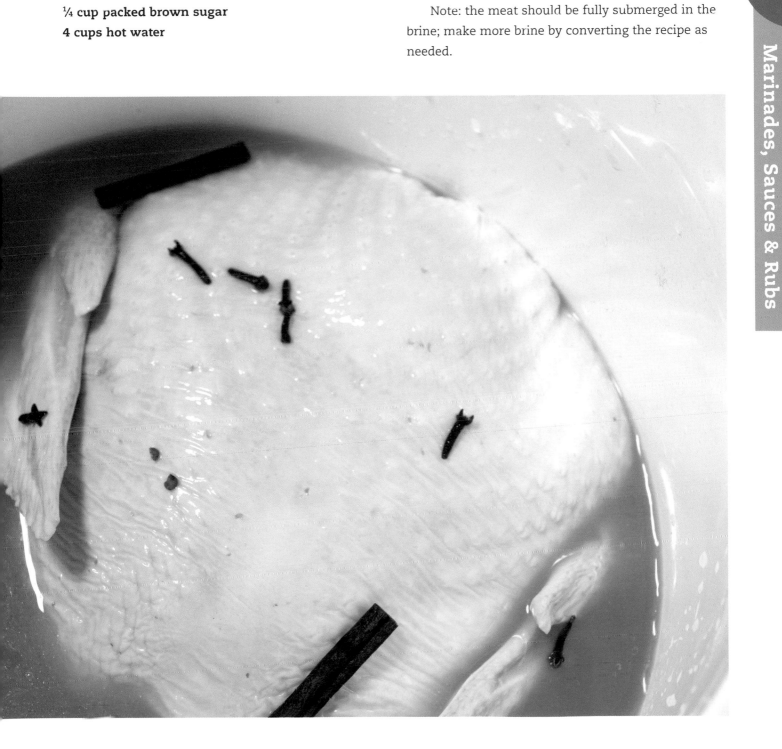

# Chipotle Marinade

Yield: ½ cup
Prep: 5–10 min.
Marinate: 2 hr.–overnight
Use with: chicken

⅓ cup fresh lime juice
¼ cup fresh chopped cilantro
1 tablespoon packed brown sugar
2 teaspoons minced chipotle chilies in adobo sauce
2 tablespoons adobo sauce (from chilies)
2 cloves garlic, minced

Combine ingredients well; then pour marinade over poultry. Marinate in a plastic ziplock bag or covered dish in the refrigerator.

*This Southwestern marinade is great for chicken.—CB*

# Adobo Marinade

*Adobo means seasoning or marinade in Spanish. This dark-red marinade is often used in Filipino and Puerto Rican cooking.—CB*

Yield: 1 cup
Prep: 5–10 min.
Marinate: 2 hr.–overnight
Use with: chicken

½ cup fresh orange juice
2 tablespoons lime juice
2 tablespoons wine vinegar
3 canned chipotle chilis
3 garlic cloves
2 teaspoons oregano
½ teaspoon black pepper
½ teaspoon salt
½ teaspoon ground cumin

In the bowl of a food processor, place all ingredients; puree. Place chicken in self-sealing plastic bag; add marinade.

# Quick Chimichurri Marinade

Yield: 1½ cups
Prep: 5–10 min.
Marinate: 2 hr.–overnight
Use with: poultry

¾ cup prepared, non-creamy Caesar dressing
½ cup chopped fresh parsley
¾ teaspoon crushed red pepper
Salt and pepper

Combine ingredients well; then pour marinade over meat. Marinate in a plastic ziplock bag or covered dish in the refrigerator.

*Chimichurri originated in Argentina where it is a popular accompaniment to grilled poultry.—CB*

# CB's Basic "Wet" Rub

Yield: ½ cup
Prep: 10 min.
Marinate: 20 min.
Use with: chicken,
    vegetables

1 tablespoon minced garlic
¼ cup brown sugar
⅛ teaspoon coarse salt
⅛ teaspoon fresh ground
    black pepper
1 tablespoon Worcestershire
    sauce
⅛ cup balsamic vinegar

Combine dry ingredients; add wet ingredients; mix again. Apply to meat about 20 minutes before slow cooking. Note: use plastic gloves or plastic sandwich bags over your hands to prevent irritation from the spices. Wet rub may be stored in the refrigerator for up to 3 days.

**6**

*This rub forms a paste when the wet and dry ingredients are mixed together. —CB*

# CB's Basic Dry Rub

Yield: 1 cup
Prep: 10 min.
Marinate: 1 hr.–overnight
Use with: chicken

½ cup garlic powder
⅛ cup kosher salt
⅛ cup powdered ginger
⅛ cup dry mustard

3 tablespoons coarsely ground black pepper
1 tablespoon cumin powder
½ tablespoon curry powder

Combine ingredients in a bowl; mix thoroughly with a wire whisk. Pour the rub mixture into a clean, dry jar and tightly seal. Massage 2 to 3 tablespoons of the rub into the meat. Store the remaining rub away from light and heat.

# CB's Indian Spice Rub

Yield: ½ cup
Prep: 10 min.
Use with: chicken, vegetables

1 tablespoon cumin seeds
1 tablespoon coriander seeds
1 tablespoon fennel seeds
1 tablespoon kosher salt
½ tablespoon curry powder
¼ to ½ teaspoon cayenne pepper

4 large garlic cloves
¼ cup fresh lemon juice
½ tablespoon vegetable oil

In a small, heavy skillet, toast cumin, coriander, and fennel seeds over high heat, stirring until fragrant and lightly browned (about 2 minutes). Cool on a plate. Place seeds in blender, and whirl until finely ground. Add salt, curry powder, cayenne, and garlic; blend to a paste. Add lemon juice and oil; blend to combine.

# CB's Dry Sugar Rub

Yield: ¼ cup
Prep: 10 min.
Use with: chicken

2 tablespoons sugar
1 tablespoon chili powder
1 teaspoon black pepper
½ tablespoon ground cumin
½ tablespoon paprika

½ tablespoon salt
¼ teaspoon dry mustard
Dash of cinnamon

Combine ingredients in a bowl; mix thoroughly with a wire whisk. Pour the rub mixture into a clean, dry jar, and tightly seal. Massage 2 to 3 tablespoons of the rub into the meat. Store the remaining rub away from light and heat.

# CB's Southwest-Style Rub

Yield: 1 cup
Prep: 10 min.
Marinate: 20 min.
Use with: chicken

## DRY INGREDIENTS

¼ cup chili powder
¼ cup packed brown sugar
⅛ cup ground cumin
⅛ cup kosher salt
⅛ cup black pepper
1 teaspoon ground cinnamon

## WET INGREDIENTS

1 tablespoon Worcestershire
   sauce
⅛ cup apple cider vinegar
1 tablespoon minced fresh garlic
   (or 1 tablespoon garlic powder)
1 teaspoon hot sauce

Mix the dry ingredients; add the wet ingredients; mix again. Store mixture in the refrigerator for up to 3 days. Apply the rub to meat; let meat rest for about 20 minutes before slow cooking. Note: use plastic gloves or plastic sandwich bags over your hands to prevent irritation from the spices.

**6**

*I developed this rub to please guests who enjoy something a little spicy. I think it works well with just about any meat, but particularly with chicken when rubbed on about 20 minutes or so before you start the slow-cooking process."—CB*

# CB's Teriyaki-Style Sauce

Yield: ¾ cup
Prep: 5–10 min.
Use with: chicken, vegetables

½ cup firmly packed dark brown sugar
½ cup soy sauce
¼ cup of hot water (or more to taste)
1 tablespoon Asian sesame oil
1 teaspoon dry Chinese-style mustard
1 teaspoon ground ginger
1 teaspoon orange zest

Combine the ingredients in saucepan. Heat, and brush on meat during final minutes of grilling.

*Teryaki sauce is a great finishing touch for almost any grilled food, especially chicken—even vegetables.*—CB

# CB's Basic Beer Sauce

Yield: 3 cups
Prep: 15 min.
Use with: poultry

1 12-ounce can or bottle of ale or dark beer
½ cup apple cider
½ cup water
¼ cup peanut oil
2 medium shallots, chopped
3 garlic cloves, chopped
1 tablespoon Worcestershire sauce
1 teaspoon hot sauce

Combine the ingredients in a saucepan. Heat the mixture, and brush it on the meat during the final minutes of grilling.

*Beer seems to be plentiful around many backyard barbecues. Try using a richer beer to make this excellent "mop" for your low- and slow-cooking barbecue or grilled meats.*—CB

# North Carolina BBQ Sauce I

Yield: 2 cups
Prep: 15 min.
Marinate: 2 hr.
Use with: chicken

2 cups cider vinegar
¼ cup brown sugar
1 tablespoon crushed red pepper

3 teaspoons salt
1½ teaspoons ground cayenne chili
1 teaspoon freshly ground black pepper
1 teaspoon ground white pepper

Combine all ingredients in a large bowl; mix well; and let stand for 2 hours to blend the flavors.

# North Carolina BBQ Sauce II

Yield: 2 cups
Prep: 15 min.
Use with: chicken

2 cups cider vinegar
¼ cup brown sugar
1 tablespoon crushed red pepper
3 teaspoons salt
1½ teaspoons ground cayenne chili
1 teaspoon freshly ground black pepper

1 teaspoon ground white pepper
1 cup ketchup
1 teaspoon Worcestershire sauce
½ teaspoon cinnamon

Combine all ingredients in a large bowl; mix well; and let stand for 2 hours to blend the flavors.

# Memphis BBQ Sauce

Yield: 3 cups
Prep: 15 min.
Cook: 25 min.
Use with: chicken

¼ cup apple cider vinegar
½ cup prepared mustard
2 cups ketchup
3 tablespoons Worcestershire sauce
1 tablespoon finely ground black pepper
¼ cup brown sugar
2 teaspoons celery salt
2 tablespoons chili powder
1 tablespoon onion powder
2 teaspoons garlic powder

¼ to ½ teaspoon cayenne pepper (optional)
2 teaspoons liquid smoke (optional)
2 tablespoons canola oil

Combine all ingredients, except the oil, in a saucepan. Bring them to a boil, stirring to dissolve the sugar. Reduce the heat, and simmer for 25 minutes, stirring occasionally. With a whisk, blend in the oil until incorporated.

# Texas BBQ Sauce

Yield: 3 cups (enough for 6 pounds of meat)
Prep: 15 min.
Cook: 20 min.
Use with: poultry

1 tablespoon salt
1 teaspoon barbecue seasoning mix
½ teaspoon pepper
3 tablespoons brown sugar
¼ cup ketchup
½ cup Worcestershire sauce
3 tablespoons Dijon mustard
1 tablespoon liquid smoke

1 cup brewed, strong coffee
½ cup vinegar
1 cup olive oil

Mix the ingredients in the order given, using a hand-held mixer when adding the oil. Simmer slowly until thickened. Keep hot. Use to baste poultry.

# South Carolina Red BBQ Sauce

**Yield: 2 cups**
**Prep: 20 min.**
**Use with: chicken**

1½ cups apple cider vinegar
½ cup ketchup
1 tablespoon brown sugar
1 teaspoon salt
½ teaspoon crushed red pepper

Combine all the ingredients; stir until sugar and salt dissolve. Taste, and adjust the sauce by adding more ketchup and brown sugar to reduce the tangy flavor. Sauce can be prepared up to 3 days ahead; covered; and refrigerated.

# CB's EZ Dr. Pepper BBQ Sauce

Yield: 3 cups
Prep: 10 min.
Cook: 10 min.
Use with: chicken

12 ounces regular Dr. Pepper
1 cup tomato ketchup
¼ cup apple cider vinegar
¼ cup Worcestershire sauce
⅛ teaspoon hot pepper sauce
2 tablespoons CB's Basic Dry Rub
(See page 154.)
2 teaspoons paprika

Combine Dr. Pepper, ketchup, vinegar, Worcestershire, and hot pepper sauce in a saucepan on your grill's side burner; bring mixture to just below a boil. Stirring gently, mix in the dry ingredients. Bring to a boil. Brush the mixture on during grilling, or serve as a dipping sauce.

*Hot Dr. Pepper is served at the soft-drink company's headquarters during the winter months. I like to drink the cold variety when I grill, and I started adding it to some homemade sauces a few years ago. Use this as a mop sauce, glaze, or dipping sauce for chicken.—CB*

**6**

Marinades, Sauces & Rubs

# Reverend Stephen's Temptation BBQ Sauce

Yield: 3½ cups
Prep: 15 min.
Cook: 20 min.
Use with: smoked or
    barbecued chicken

*This recipe was sent to CB by a BBQ fan known as Reverend Stephen.*

½ onion, minced
4 garlic cloves, minced
¾ cup bourbon
½ teaspoon ground black
    pepper
½ tablespoon salt
2 cups ketchup
¼ cup tomato paste
⅓ cup apple cider vinegar
2 tablespoons liquid smoke
¼ cup Worcestershire sauce
¼ cup packed brown sugar
½ teaspoon hot pepper sauce
    (or to taste)

In a large skillet over medium heat, combine the onion, garlic, and bourbon. Simmer for 10 minutes or until the onion is translucent. Mix in the ground black pepper, salt, ketchup, tomato paste, vinegar, liquid smoke, Worcestershire sauce, brown sugar, and hot pepper sauce. Bring this to a boil. Reduce the heat to medium-low, and simmer for 20 minutes. If you prefer a smoother sauce, pour the mixture through a strainer.

# CB's Georgia-Style Mustard Sauce

Yield: 2½ cups
Prep: 10 min.
Cook: 20–30 min.
Use with: chicken

2 tablespoons vegetable oil
½ cup minced Vidalia or other sweet onion
1 cup prepared mustard
½ cup fresh lemon juice (or lemonade)
¼ cup firmly packed dark brown sugar

¼ cup apple cider vinegar
1 teaspoon celery seed
1 teaspoon kosher salt
1 teaspoon powdered ginger

Heat the oil in a nonreactive saucepan over medium heat. Add the onions, and sauté until translucent, about 3 to 4 minutes. Add the rest of the ingredients; blend well. Bring the mixture to a boil; then reduce the heat and simmer for 15 to 20 minutes.

# CB's Lemon-Garlic Butter Sauce

Yield: ¼ cup per serving
Prep: 15 min.
Cook: 5 min.
Use with: chicken, vegetables

**PER SERVING**

2 tablespoons clarified butter (See note.)
½ fresh lemon, juiced
2 tablespoons light olive oil or canola oil
1 garlic clove, crushed
¼ teaspoon lemon zest

Combine the ingredients in a saucepan. Heat the mixture, and brush it on food during the final minutes of grilling and on the serving plate.

*Clarified butter has a higher smoke point than regular butter. Place 1 pound of unsalted butter in a saucepan at the back of the stove; cover; and allow the butter to melt while you're cooking. Skim off the solids that have risen to the surface. Use immediately, or pour into a glass container to freeze.* —CB

# CB's Tarragon-Butter Sauce

Yield: ¼ cup per serving
Prep: 10 min.
Use with: chicken, vegetables

**PER SERVING**

2 tablespoons clarified butter (See note above.)
2 tablespoons light olive oil or canola oil
1 tablespoon chopped fresh tarragon

Combine all ingredients in a saucepan. Heat the mixture, and brush it on chicken or vegetables during the final minutes of grilling.

# Roasted Garlic

Yield: about ¼ cup
Prep: 5–10 min.
Cook: 30–40 min. on the grill, 35–45 min.
    in the oven
Use with: chicken, grilled corn, or
    as a spread on grilled bruschetta

**1 whole garlic bulb**
**1 teaspoon canola oil**
**1 small rosemary sprig (optional)**
**Freshly ground black pepper to taste**
**Salt to taste (optional)**

Cut ½ inch off the top of the garlic bulb so that individual cloves are exposed. Cut an 8-inch-square sheet of heavy-duty aluminum foil. Place the garlic bulb on the foil; add oil to the cut end of the garlic bulb. Place the herb sprig across the bulb, and season with pepper and salt. Wrap foil around the bulb.

Preheat the grill to high. When ready, place the wrapped bulb on the grill and cook for 30 to 40 minutes, turning carefully several times.

Remove the bulb from the grill; let cool. Squeeze the cooked garlic bulb by hand, and the delicious, soft pulp will come forth. If desired, the garlic can be roasted in the oven at 375°F for 45 minutes to 1 hour until soft.

# Roasted-Garlic Mayo

Yield: 1 cup
Prep: 20 min.
Use with: chicken, vegetables

**2 whole heads roasted garlic (See recipe above.)**
**1 cup prepared mayonnaise**
**½ teaspoon lemon juice**

Squeeze garlic pulp from cloves into the work bowl of a food processor; pulse three or four times until smooth. Add the mayonnaise and lemon juice, and blend until smooth and well combined. Use this mayonnaise immediately, or cover and refrigerate for up to 2 days.

# Better-than-Homemade Mayo

Yield: 1 cup
Prep: 20 min.
Use with: chicken

**1 cup prepared mayonnaise**
**1½ tablespoons olive oil**
**¼ teaspoon fresh lemon juice**
**¼ teaspoon minced garlic**
**Tabasco sauce to taste**

Whisk the ingredients together. This mayonnaise can be used immediately, or covered and refrigerated for 2 to 3 weeks.

# Roasted Red-Pepper Mayo

Yield: 1¼ cups
Prep: 20 min.
Use with: chicken,
   vegetables

**2 red peppers, roasted and
   chopped**
**1 garlic clove, chopped**
**1 cup prepared mayonnaise**
**¼ teaspoon cayenne pepper**

Combine the peppers and garlic in a food processor; blend until smooth. Add the mayonnaise and cayenne until combined. Use this mayonnaise immediately, or cover and refrigerate for up to 2 days.

# CB's Orange Aioli

Yield: 1¼ cups
Prep: 10 min.
Use with: chicken, vegetables

1 cup mayonnaise
¼ cup orange juice
1 tablespoon hot-pepper sauce
½ teaspoon sugar
½ teaspoon chopped garlic
½ teaspoon prepared horseradish
2 tablespoons chopped scallions

Stir all ingredients together and refrigerate until ready to use. Because it only keeps for a few days, make just enough to use in about 24 hours.

*Aioli is a word that has been popping up on restaurant menus all over the place. It's really just flavored mayonnaise. So whether you make your own mayo or purchase it in jars like most folks, experiment with some new flavors and impress your friends when you call it aioli. (A-OH-LEE!)—CB*

# Guacamole

Yield: about 2 cups
Prep: 15 min., plus 1 hr.
　refrigeration
Use with: taco chips,
　raw vegetables

3 to 4 large, ripe avocados
5 cloves roasted garlic
　(See page 162.)
Juice of 1 lime
2 tablespoons chopped cilantro
½ teaspoon red pepper flakes
Salt and pepper to taste
1 large tomato, diced

Peel the avocados; discard the pits; and remove any bad spots. Cut them into ½-inch cubes. In a food processor, blend together the avocado, garlic, lime juice, cilantro, red pepper, and salt and pepper. Move to a serving dish. Stir in the chopped tomato. Cover, and refrigerate for 1 hour.

# Classic Parmesan-Basil Pesto

Yield: about 2 cups
Prep: 5–10 min.
Use with: chicken breast,
　vegetables

1⅓ cups basil leaves
1½ teaspoons chopped garlic
¼ cup pine nuts, toasted
½ cup grated Parmesan cheese
¼ cup olive oil
Salt and pepper to taste

Combine first four ingredients in a food processor; pulse three or four times. With motor running, slowly drizzle in olive oil until mixture blends into a paste. Season with salt and pepper to taste.

# Sun-Dried Tomato Pesto

Yield: about 2 cups
Prep: 5–10 min.
Use with: chicken breast,
　vegetables

1½ cups sun-dried tomatoes,
　packed in oil, drained
6 garlic cloves, peeled
1 cup grated Parmesan cheese
1 cup fresh basil leaves
½ cup olive oil
2 tablespoons balsamic vinegar

Combine all ingredients in a food processor or blender; blend until mixture is smooth and well combined.

# Plum Marinade

Yield: approx. ¾ cup
Prep: 5 min.
Marinate: 4–6 hr.
Use with: chicken

½ cup plum preserves
3 tablespoons minced green onion
2 tablespoons white vinegar
2 tablespoons hoisin sauce
2 teaspoons minced fresh ginger
1 teaspoon dry mustard
½ teaspoon crushed red pepper

In a bowl, whisk together all ingredients until completely emulsified. Marinate meat in a sealable plastic bag or covered container in the refrigerator.

# Three-Way Marinade

Yield: 1 cup
Prep: 5 min.
Marinate: 4–12 hr.
Use with: poultry

## CLASSIC MARINADE

1 cup prepared Italian-style vinaigrette
1 teaspoon minced garlic
¼ teaspoon coarsely ground black pepper

## MEXICAN VARIATION

To classic marinade, add
1 tablespoon fresh lime juice
1 teaspoon ground cumin
1 teaspoon chipotle chili powder
½ teaspoon salt

## ASIAN VARIATION

To classic marinade, add
2 tablespoons reduced-sodium soy sauce
2 tablespoons minced fresh ginger
1 tablespoon packed brown sugar
1 tablespoon sesame seeds, toasted
1½ teaspoons dark sesame oil

In a bowl, whisk together all ingredients until completely emulsified. Marinate meat in a sealable plastic bag or covered container in the refrigerator.

# Captain Jessie's Jamaican Jerk Marinade

Yield: 1 cup
Prep: 10 min.
Marinate: 4 hr.–overnight
Use with: poultry

1 white onion, chopped
½ cup chopped scallions
2 teaspoons fresh thyme
or
1 teaspoon dried thyme

*Spices from the Caribbean give this marinade a kick to heat up your mouth!*

1 whole Scotch Bonnet or habanero pepper, seeded and chopped
1 teaspoon coarse salt
2 teaspoons light brown sugar
1 teaspoon allspice
½ teaspoon ground nutmeg
½ teaspoon ground cinnamon
1 teaspoon black pepper
1 tablespoon soy sauce
1 tablespoon Worcestershire sauce
1 tablespoon vegetable oil
1 tablespoon apple cider vinegar

In a food processor or blender, add the onions, scallions, thyme, and peppers. Stir in the other ingredients, and pulse until mixture becomes a light slurry. Marinate meat in a sealable plastic bag or covered container in the refrigerator.

**NOTE:** when working with fresh peppers, use food-safe gloves; do not touch your eyes, mouth, or nose until you have washed your hands with soap and water.

# Jan's Dry Rub

Yield: approx. 3 cups
Prep: 5 min.
Use with: chicken

1¼ cups sugar
¼ cup Lawry's
   seasoned salt
¼ cup garlic salt
¼ cup + 1½ teaspoon
   celery salt
¼ cup onion salt
½ cup paprika

3 tablespoons chili powder
2 tablespoons black pepper
1 tablespoon lemon pepper
2 teaspoons celery seed
2 teaspoons ground dry sage
1 teaspoon dry mustard
½ teaspoon ground dry thyme
½ teaspoon cayenne pepper

Blend all ingredients in a
large bowl.

*"Sizzle on the Grill" contributor KyNola says his wife,
Jan, came up with this recipe to match a secret version
at a local BBQ restaurant. It has "only" 14 ingredients
and makes a bunch.*

# Chili-Cinnamon Rub for Chicken

Yield: approx. ¼ cup
Prep: 5 min.
Use with: chicken

2 teaspoons ancho chili powder
2 teaspoons ground cinnamon
2 teaspoons ground cumin
4 teaspoons fresh thyme
2 teaspoons salt
2 teaspoons brown sugar

Blend the spices, salt, and sugar
in a small bowl.

*Ancho chili powder works well in this recipe, but you can
use chipotle or other, milder chili powders.*

# Spicy Grilled-Veggie Marinade

Yield: 1½ cups
Prep: 5 min.
Marinate: 1 hr.
Use with: vegetables

⅔ cup white wine vinegar
½ cup soy sauce
2 tablespoons minced fresh
   ginger
2 tablespoons olive oil
2 tablespoons sesame oil
2 large cloves garlic, minced
2 teaspoons Tabasco sauce

In a bowl, whisk together all ingredients until completely emulsified. Marinate in a sealable plastic bag or covered container in the refrigerator.

# Jalapeños in Adobo Sauce

Yield: 3 cups
Prep: 10–15 min.
Use with: poultry

10 jalapeño peppers, smoked
   or grilled, split, and seeded
1 can (18 ounces) tomatoes,
   diced
10 large garlic cloves, crushed
   and minced
6 tablespoons olive oil

2 tablespoons chopped fresh
   coriander or cilantro
2 tablespoons apple cider vinegar
1 tablespoon crushed red pepper
1 teaspoon cumin
1 teaspoon oregano
1 teaspoon coarse salt
Juice from ½ large lime
Juice from ½ large lemon
Pinch of brown sugar, if
   necessary

After preparing the jalapeño peppers, mix all ingredients, and seal in nonreactive container. Sauce can be kept in the refrigerator for several weeks.

# Resources

*This list of manufacturers and associations is meant to be a general guide to additional industry and product-related sources. It is not intended as a listing of all of the products and manufacturers presented in this book.*

## Companies and Associations

### CHAR-BROIL

www.charbroil.com
This is the official Web site for the Char-Broil company.

### CHICKEN FARMERS OF CANADA

www.chicken.ca
The Chicken Farmers of Canada offer nutritional and food-safety tips, recipes, and information on its Web site.

### CHRISTOPHER RANCH

www.christopherranch.com
Christopher Ranch provides product information and recipes on its Web site.

### MEN IN APRONS

www.meninaprons.net
This Web site is dedicated to all things cooking and grilling related.

### OCEAN MIST FARMS

www.oceanmist.com
Ocean Mist Farms provides recipes, videos, and nutrition information on its Web site.

### SIZZLE ON THE GRILL

www.sizzleonthegrill.com
Char-Broil sponsors this newsletter and Web site, which features grilling tips and recipes.

### UNITED STATES DEPARTMENT OF AGRICULTURE (USDA) FOOD SAFETY AND INSPECTION SERVICE

www.fsis.usda.gov
The Web site offers consumer safety information on buying, storing, preparing, and cooking meat and poultry.

### USDA MEAT & POULTRY HOTLINE

888-MPHotline
This hotline answers questions about safe storage, handling, and preparation of meat and poultry products.

## Food Blogs and Recipe Databases

### DANICA'S DAILY

http://danicasdaily.com
This blog focuses on recipes for a healthy lifestyle.

### DIANASAUR DISHES

www.dianasaurdishes.com
Diana Johnson shares recipes for healthy meals that are affordable and easy to make.

### MARCIA'S KITCHEN

www.happyinthekitchen.com
Marcia Frankenberg lives in Minneapolis, where her main inspiration for cooking is hearing her daughter say, "Feed me, Mama!"

### NOT EATING OUT IN NEW YORK

www.noteatingoutinny.com
Cathy Erway is the author of *The Art of Eating In: How I Learned to Stop Spending and Love the Stove,* which is based on her two-year mission to forego restaurant food, and her blog, which is filled with original recipes for the busy-but-thrifty.

## "Sizzle on the Grill" Contributors

### THE BBQ GRAIL

http://thebbqgrail.com
Larry Gaian, food author, posts recipes and barbecue information on his site.

### GIRLS ON A GRILL

www.girlsonagrill.com
These guest chefs are sisters who share their recipes featuring fresh ingredients cooked over an open fire.

### LIVEFIRE

http://livefireonline.com
Curt McAdams explores barbecuing and grilling, in addition to local foods and markets, breads, and other baking.

# Index

Have a home gardening, decorating, or improvement project?
Look for these and other fine **Creative Homeowner** books
wherever books are sold

**ULTIMATE GUIDE TO OUTDOOR PROJECTS**
Hardscape and landscape projects that add value and enjoyment to your home.

Over 1,200 photographs and illustrations.
368 pp.
8½" × 10⅞"
$19.95 (US)
$23.95 (CAN)
BOOK #: CH277873

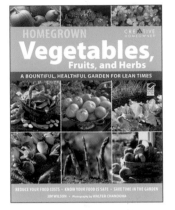

**HOMEGROWN VEGETABLES**
A complete guide to growing your own vegetables, fruits, and herbs.

Over 275 photographs and illustrations.
192 pp.
8½" × 10⅞"
$16.95 (US)
$20.95 (CAN)
BOOK #: CH274551

**3 STEP VEGETABLE GARDENING**
A quick and easy guide for growing your own fruit and vegetables.

Over 300 photographs.
224 pp.
8½" × 10⅞"
$19.95 (US)
$21.95 (CAN)
BOOK #: CH274557

**SUCCESSFUL CONTAINER GARDENING**
Information to grow your own flower, fruit, and vegetable "gardens."

Over 240 photographs.
160 pp.
8½" × 10⅞"
$14.95 (US)
$17.95 (CAN)
BOOK #: CH274857

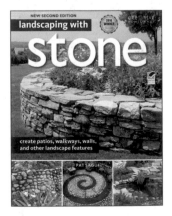

**LANDSCAPING WITH STONE**
Ideas for incorporating stone into the landscape.

Over 335 photographs.
224 pp.
8½" × 10⅞"
$19.95 (US)
$21.95 (CAN)
BOOK #: CH274179

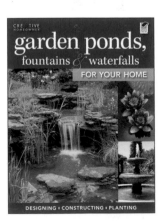

**GARDEN PONDS, FOUNTAINS & WATERFALLS FOR YOUR HOME**
Secrets to creating garden water features.

Over 490 photographs and illustrations.
256 pp.
8½" × 10⅞"
$19.95 (US)
$22.95 (CAN)
BOOK #: CH274450

For more information and to order direct, go to **www.creativehomeowner.com**